The New York Times

Country Music's Greatest Songs

93 songs arranged for *piano, voice and guitar*

Edited by Milton Okun

Times
BOOKS

Acknowledgments:

Once again I must thank a most valuable and competent team of associates for their assistance and resourcefulness: Jean Dinegar, Dan Fox, Lauren Keiser, Pat Raven and Mary Ann Tiernan-O'Grady. As to Messrs. Tom Lipscomb, Len Schwartz and Murray Frank, their encouragement and prodding really paid off with not one but two books of the greatest songs—Country Music's and those very special remembrances of the Seventies!

Also, my appreciation to those publishers who have cooperated so generously in making this collection possible.

Milton Okun

781
0

Published by TIMES BOOKS, a division of
Quadrangle/The New York Times Book Co., Inc.
Three Park Avenue, New York, N.Y. 10016
Published simultaneously in Canada by
Fitzhenry & Whiteside, Ltd., Toronto.

Copyright © 1978 by Milton Okun

Library of Congress Catalog Card Number: 78-58169
International Standard Book Number: 0-8129-0791-4

Manufactured in the United States of America.

Photographs courtesy of *The New York Times.*

Contents

IV

Introduction

To take the long view, *The New York Times Country Music's Greatest Songs* is the result of three great historic events and a whole lot of harmless musical fooling around during idle times.

The first great historic event took place in the Eighteenth Century when the British Government attempted to disperse the Scottish Tribes after the Jacobean uprisings of 1715 (The Old Pretender) and 1745 (Bonnie Prince Charlie). Many Scots, discouraged by the English attempts to stop border raids and border contraband, had already moved to Ireland. Here they found the colleens congenial, but the English laws still intolerable. In the latter part of the century there was a great movement of Scots and Irish, and Scots-Irish to the New World where they found the New England Anglicans not only in possession of all the good land but as unreceptive to their Calvinist ways as had been the British themselves.

And so they pushed on, these Scots-Irish, taking with them what little they had: a proud heritage of independence, a few iron pots, a spotted hog, and their music. Sometimes they managed to bring a musical instrument too, but these were hard times, naked times, and if the choice came between a kid or a piglet or a bagpipe, the bagpipe was left behind.

Through the Cumberland Gap they came and spread out through the hill country of Kentucky and Tennessee, of North and South Carolina. Tragically unaware of the richness of this new world, they frequently chose the wrong site for the family farm, ignoring the rich bottom lands in favor of the thin-soiled highlands (The Ridge Runners), or settling in barren hollows that reminded them of the Scottish Highlands. Here they settled in proud isolation in a land that was already oriented toward the West, toward the abundances of gold and the fertility of the Middle Border.

Their Fundamentalist beliefs supported them in their poverty and isolation *(Amazing Grace)*, but these same beliefs also contributed to their troubles: too many children on a small farm, for example. The drain of manpower to the city began early. The father might in despair take to drink *(Please Daddy, Don't Get Drunk This Christmas)*, or simply desert to the jobs in the city. If the father didn't go then the older sons did…and all of this is recorded in their music. It is a music filled with longing, nostalgia, sorrow and lamentation for a lost Eden of childhood *(Take Me Home, Country Roads)*. But never despair! There is not only the sound of saving grace in their music, there is endemic to it a unique country humor.

The Country Rube is hanging on the split-rail fence
when the City Feller sluffs up.
"Hey, how long until I get to the next town?"
But the Rube doesn't answer, just stands there with
his wrists dangling down.
"To hell," says the City Feller and starts off. At
the edge of the property, the Rube calls him back.
"An hour and a half to the next town," he says.
"Why didn't you tell me that before?"
"I didn't know how fast you could walk."

There it is, caught in a joke, the pride, the independence, the isolation, the humor, and the Fundamentalist belief in *truth.*

During this time of isolation the country folk developed their own music and new musical instruments. Music was required for hoedowns and harvest festivals and marriage celebrations; but there were the everyday occupations that required song, too: cradle rocking, butter churning, plowing and game playing. Because of the isolation of the people who created them, the country songs retained an Elizabethan flavor, although they were adapted to new musical instruments: the five-string banjo, the harmonica and the dulcimer.

World War II was the second great historical event that changed the course of country music. That war changed the face of the Western Hemisphere, so, of course, it made its impact on country music, too. One can say with some precision what World War II did for country music: It wasn't a change in music or theme or instrumentation; World War II gave country music a national audience.

Before the war, when rural boys had migrated to the cities they had been in search of jobs and they had either hunkered down in some comfortably rural suburb, or they had divested themselves of rural ways, rural music and overalls, to compete for the jobs available to them *(Detroit City)*. The young men who were drafted in wartime saw no reason to camouflage their origin. They were in for the duration; they would fight as their daddies had done in the Great War (Sergeant Alvin York was honored at the premiere of the 1940 movie *The Grand Ole Opry)*, and then they would return to their hollers and farms. There was no need to seek camouflage; they brought with them into the army their music, their instruments, their Fundamentalist beliefs and their humor.

At induction centers and training camps, the hillbilly suddenly emerged. At one induction camp a country boy sat at the head of the line. He sat on the floor, his legs stretched out in front of him in a country manner, and he thoughtfully fingered the day's growth of his beard. "I thought to shave before I came," he announced loudly, "but then I thought to wait till after I was inducted and so do it on company time." The hillbilly had come out of the holler.

Country music was heard in army camps all over America, on North Atlantic transports, in staging camps in England and, finally, on the European Continent itself. American Forces Air Stations played *The Wabash Cannonball.*

There was a reverse movement, too. Hundreds of thousands of urban boys found themselves encamped at southern army bases. At Fort Bragg and Fort Benning, where the local radios played country music, the soldier boys from the Bronx and Berkeley might find themselves humming *Roving Gambler* as they shaved. And after the war, not all the country boys returned to their hollers. As a guess, something like ninety-nine percent of the country boys stationed at Lowery Field outside of Denver, Colorado, returned to Denver to live after the war: blue skies, federal jobs, and a Rocky Mountain high.

Henry J. Deutschendorf, Jr., chose his singing name wisely: John Denver. He is in the mainstream of the new country music that is the result of the third historic event: the introduction of the transistor radio.

Isolation was swept away by the transistor radio. Whereas the wartime dislocation of the population brought country music to the city, the transistor radio brought city music to the hollers. The country boys who had heard only the music of their daddies and of the courtesy uncles (Uncle Dave Macon, for instance) suddenly heard in the hollers Honky-Tonk, Rock and Roll, and the strange folk music of Harry Belafonte singing the Jamaican *Come, Tally Me Bananas.* Country music has never been the same.

But the strength of the traditional country music is shown in this collection; country music has *absorbed* innovations—Swing, Honky-Tonk, Western and Rock and Roll rhythms, and electronic amplification—and yet country music has remained true to the spirit of its origins. The songs in this collection are not very much like the songs that Alan Lomax collected when he first penetrated the Appalachians looking for *folk* music, but these songs are legitimate heirs of that music.

That music was caught and preserved for us all as some kind of a national monument by Alan Lomax, who, as a graduate student at Harvard under the tutelage of George Lyman Kitteridge, came first to wonder at what Bishop Percy had done in the Eighteenth Century in collecting the Border Ballads of Scotland and England. Together, graduate student and professor came to the realization that there was the opportunity in the isolated Appalachians to reproduce Bishop Percy's experience in collecting traditional songs. But they had a new and thrilling instrument: the Edison Recording Machine. Alan Lomax, a recording machine strapped on his back, heavy wet-cell batteries carried in either hand, slogged through the hollers and climbed the ridges, recording songs that were still truly Elizabethan and still sung in the Seventeenth Century manner, the body tightly held, the voices tight and pitched so high that some men sang a falsetto. The style has changed, but the songs are true to the source in their melodic ornamentation and in their themes. Like so many of the songs of a simple people, *Ode to Billy Joe* speaks of death and separation and unrequited love, just as did *Bonny Barbara Allen,* collected by Bishop Percy in the Eighteenth Century and again by Alan Lomax in the Twentieth.

> O mother, mother make my bed!
> O make it soft and narrow!
> My love has died for me today,
> I'll die for him tomorrow.

Unrequited love is the theme of *Another Somebody Done Somebody Wrong Song, Linda on My Mind* and *Today I Started Loving You Again.* Sometimes the longing of such love turns to sentimentality, but sometimes it turns to violence, too, and that brings us to another common theme of country music: the wandering outlaw. In the Seventeenth Century it was Robin Hood:

> Come, listen to me, you gallants so free,
> All you that loves mirth for to hear,
> And I will tell you of a bold outlaw,
> That lived in Nottinghamshire.

In the Twentieth Century it could be the violent lover, the roving gambler, the anti-establishment outlaw (Dillinger, Bonnie and Clyde), or the rootless hobo driven by poverty as in the *The Wabash Cannonball.*

> Listen to the jingle, the rumble and the roar,
> Riding through the woodlands to the hills and by the shore.
> Hear the mighty rush of the engine, hear the lonesome hobo squall,
> Riding through the jungle on the Wabash Cannonball.

But the establishment is, after all, in charge of things and doesn't, by and large, approve of the romantic outlaw, so the next great theme in country music is the prison song—a natural consequence of the previous theme. *Folsom Prison Blues* is one such song; other songs not in this collection are *Columbus Jailhouse* and *Midnight Special.* Johnny Cash's famous recording of *A Boy Named Sue* was made in Folsom Prison before an audience of prisoners, and the real electricity, the excitement of that recording, lies in the audience's wildly approving response. Whoops of pleasure and thunderous applause mark the audience's recognition of itself in the "scalawag father," in the "avenging son" and in the "barroom battlers" fighting in "the mud and the blood and the beer." Near the end of the recording, Johnny Cash identifies himself with the prisoners by stepping out of line, by deliberately breaking a broadcasting taboo, to sing of "the (bleep) that named me Sue." The laughter is generous, but the climax of the audience reaction comes at the very end of the song where hard-earned common sense and folk wisdom wins out over tricky rationalization. "If I have a son, I'm gonna name him...Bill or George, or anything but Sue."

Love of the land is one of the most enduring of the country music themes; sometimes it is combined with a nostalgia for the simple ways of remembered childhood *(Oklahoma Hills),* but sometimes there is a wry, humorous note that acknowledges the hardships of country living, and still plumps for that life as the best, *Thank God I'm A Country Boy* and *Everything Is Beautiful.* Sometimes the love of the land gets mixed up with the country ways of Fundamentalist religion and conservative politics and then there emerges the proud, flaunting satire of an *Okie from Muskogee.*

Of course, there have been changes in the music and in the themes. Some of the changes are obvious: The railroad has disappeared as a romantic image, and Casey Jones and the hobo have given way to the trucker and the hitch-hiker. The place of women has altered, too, in country music. A generation ago, woman was still the support of man, helpmate and quiet encourager:

"That's okay," Rose would say,
"Don't you worry none.
We'll have good time by and by
When the work is done."

In recent country songs the voice of woman has sounded clearly for herself. There is little subtlety to Loretta Lynn's *Don't Come Home A-Drinkin' (With A-Lovin' on Your Mind)*. Her song *The Pill* makes a little broader statement about women's place.

But even the songs that might be seen as songs of Women's Liberation fit into the old thematic patterns. *Harper Valley PTA* is couched in modern terms but it is a marvelous example of reversed terminology. The mother, beset by the hard-nosed PTA, is in fact a female Robin Hood, a romantic outlaw, who, in a wondrous reversal, is attacking the spiritually impoverished to give spiritual riches to her child. In country music, as in everything else, everything changes but change.

It used to be said that the aristocracy and the folk shared this one thing in common: You couldn't join them; you had to be born to them. Loretta Lynn makes this point in the title of her autobiography, *Coal Miner's Daughter;* and Burke's *Peerage* remains unshaken in its belief that birth makes the difference, not talent nor wealth. But in country music there has been a change of late: Some of the leading composers and singers have not been born to the folk. Johnny Cash, Loretta Lynn, Dolly Parton and Tom T. Hall were all, as it were, to the holler born. But there are other leading composers and singers who were not born-folk: John Denver, Shel Silverstein and Kris Kristofferson, for instance.

Before World War II, the chief musical instrument of the American home was the piano. The piano dominated the living room unless the house had been specifically designed with a "music room" that would shelter the piano. Children were taught music on the piano and at Christmas and Thanksgiving relatives sat in respectful awe as the child played his greatest triumph, *Barcarolle* from Offenbach's *Tales of Hoffmann.*

The piano was the musical instrument most commonly used to accompany singers, and at parties and reunions people gathered around the piano to sing. But all this has changed sharply since country music came out of the hills. The guitar is now the instrument that most children first learn to play and it is the guitar that is the most common musical instrument played to accompany group singing.

Country music isn't the only reason for this change. American society is much more loosely constructed and mobile now: One can sling a guitar on one's back or pitch it into the back of an RV, and the television set in the living room effectively silences the piano for many hours of the day and night. But in fraternity houses, at political rallies, and in back bedrooms where adolescents cope with the problems of growing up, it is the guitar that is heard, and, often, the sounds of country music.

Thanks to those last two great historic events described earlier in this introduction one need not be born into poverty and isolation to grow up in the country tradition. The national audience and the transistor radio make it possible for a child in Minneapolis or Denver, or even New York, to grow up with those country principles of proud independence and respect for the everyday problems of the simple folk: death, poverty, separation, and unrequited love...and to see all of them countered with humor and song.

Perhaps this book, *Country Music's Greatest Songs*, represents a fourth great historic event. We are all no longer audience to country music; we can be a part of it, contributors to that great tradition. It isn't so much that country has become national; we have been able to understand and at last enjoy and contribute to one of our oldest musical heritages. *Thank God I'm A Country Boy!*

Milton Okun

3

4

1 *The Statler Brothers*
2 *Elvis Presley*
3 *John Denver*
4 *Kenny Rogers*

6

7

8

9

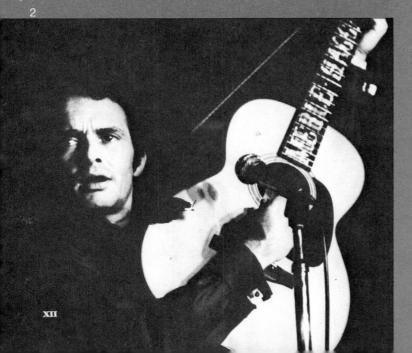

XII

(Hey, Won't You Play)
Another Somebody
Done Somebody Wrong Song

Words and Music by Larry Butler and Chips Moman

1

sad that it makes ev-'ry-bod - y cry._____

_____ A real hurt-in' song a-bout a

love that's gone___ wrong, 'Cause I don't___ wan - na

D. S. al Fine 𝄋

cry all a - lone.

Act Naturally

Words and Music by Johnny Russell and Vonie Morrison

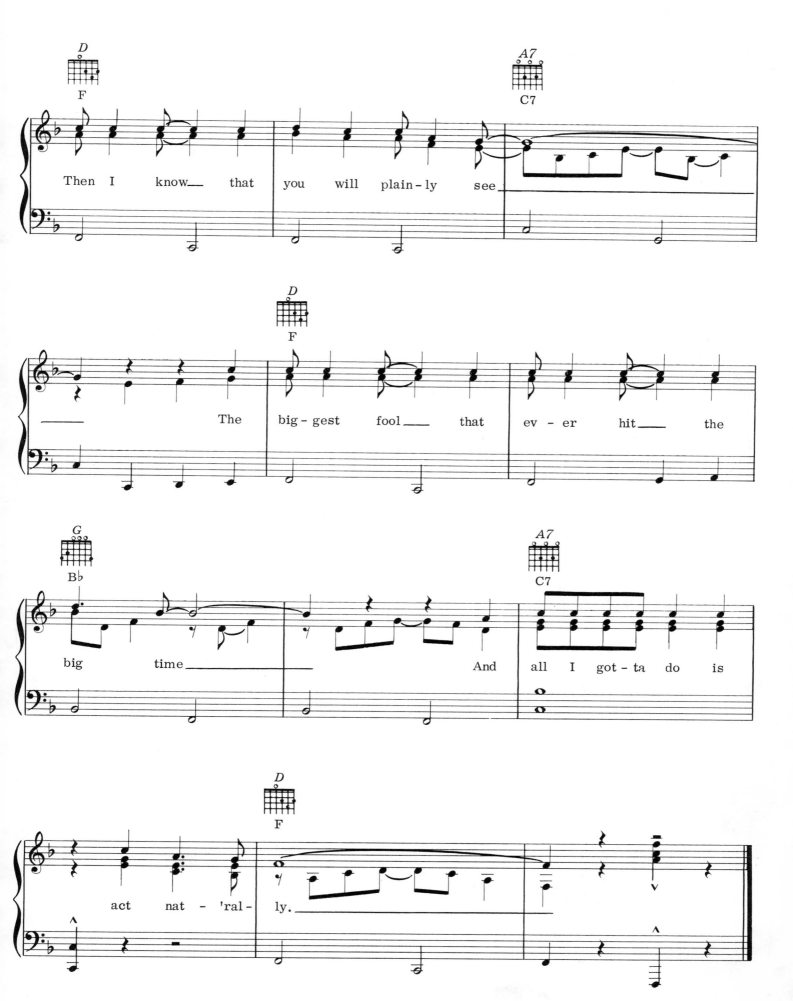

Before The Next Teardrop Falls

Moderately slow

Words and Music by Ben Peters and Vivian Keith

tear-drops ev - er start, I'll be there be-fore the next tear-drop
made you shed a tear,

1. falls.

Tho' it falls.

2. I'll be

there an - y time you need me by your side To

dry a - way ev-'ry tear-drop that you cried. If he

ev - er leaves you blue, just re - mem - ber I love

you, I'll be there be - fore the next tear - drop

falls. Yes, I'll be there be - fore the

next tear - drop falls.

Back Home Again

Words and Music by John Denver

gone.
say?
home.

There's a fire_____ soft - ly
And your moth-er_____ called last
Like a fire_____ soft - ly

burn-ing,___
Fri - day;___
burn-ing___ and

sup - per's on___ the stove___
"Sun-shine" made___ her cry,___
sup - per on___ the stove___

But it's the
And you
And the

light in your eyes___ that makes him warm.___
felt the ba - by move___ just yes - ter - day.___
light in your eyes___ that makes me warm.___

Chorus

Hey, it's good to be back home___ a - gain;___

Some-times___ this old farm___ feels___ like a long-lost

friend. Yes 'n' hey, it's good___ to be back home a-gain.___

1. There's 2. And oh, the time that

I can lay___ this tired___ old bod-y down and

15

Battle Of New Orleans

Words and Music by Jimmy Driftwood

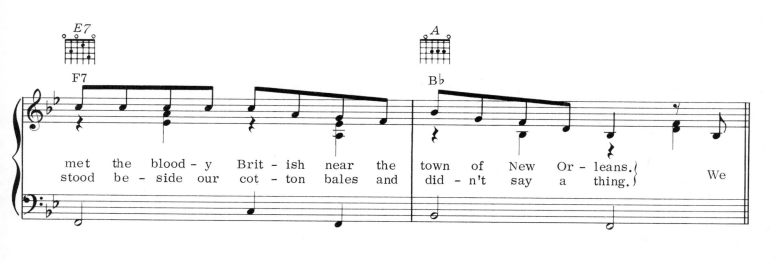

met the blood—y Brit—ish near the town of New Or—leans.
stood be—side our cot—ton bales and did—n't say a thing.

We

Chorus

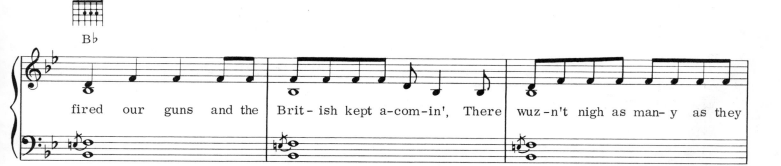

fired our guns and the Brit—ish kept a—com—in', There wuz—n't nigh as man—y as they

wuz a while a—go. We fired once more and they be—gan to run—nin', On

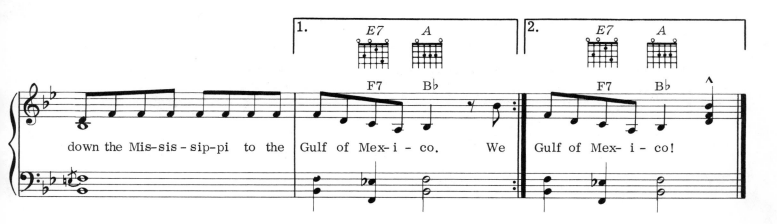

1.
down the Mis—sis—sip—pi to the Gulf of Mex—i—co. We

2.
Gulf of Mex—i—co!

17

Berkeley Woman

Slow Country feeling

Words and Music by Bryan Bowers

saw a Berke-ley wom — an ___ what my sit-tin' in her rock-in' chair,
2) hard to be-lieve ___ eyes showed me then, ___

___ a dul-ci-mer in her lap, ___ a
___ the col-or in her cheeks ___ was

feath-er in ___ her hair. ___ Her ___ breasts swayed ___
just her nat-u-ral skin. ___ She ___ wore no

3. I fin'lly realized there was hunger in my stare,
   And in my mind I was swayin' with the woman in the rockin' chair.
   But the lady I was livin' with was standin' right by my side,
   She saw me stare and she saw my hunger, and Lord, it made her cry.

4. So with anger in her face and hurt in her eyes,
   She scratched me and she clawed me, she screamed and she cried,
   "Oh, you don't give me near all the lovin' that you should,
   Yet you're ready to go and lay with her; you're just no damn good."

5. Well, I guess she's prob'ly right, I guess I'm prob'ly wrong,
   I guess she's not too far away, she hasn't been gone very long.
   And I guess we could get together and try just one more time,
   But I know that wanderlust would come again, she'd only wind up cry'n'.

6. Now you've heard this story, plain as the light of day,
   It's hard to feel guilty for lovin' the ladies, that's all I gotta say.
   'Cept a woman is the sweetest fruit that God ever put on the vine,
   And I'd no more love just one kind-a woman than drink only one kind-a (wine.)

Daddy Sang Bass

Words and Music by Carl Perkins

geth-er in a fam – 'ly cir – cle sing – in' loud._____
geth-er a – gain up yonder in a lit – tle while._____

Chorus

Dad-dy sang bass, ma-ma sang ten-or, me and lit-tle bro-ther would join right in there;

Sing-in' seems to help a trou-bled soul._____ One of these days and it won't be

long, I'll re-join them in a song; I'm gon-na join the fam-'ly cir-cle at the

throne._____ No, the cir - cle_____ won't be bro - ken,

_____ Bye and bye, Lord, bye and bye._____ Dad - dy'll sing

bass, ma - ma'll sing ten - or, me and lit-tle bro-ther will join right in there in the

sky, Lord__ in the sky._____ 2. Now I re-   sky._____

A Boy Named Sue

Words and Music by Shel Silverstein

ever did was be - fore he left, he went and named me Sue.

Verse II

2. Well, he must have thought it was quite a joke, And it

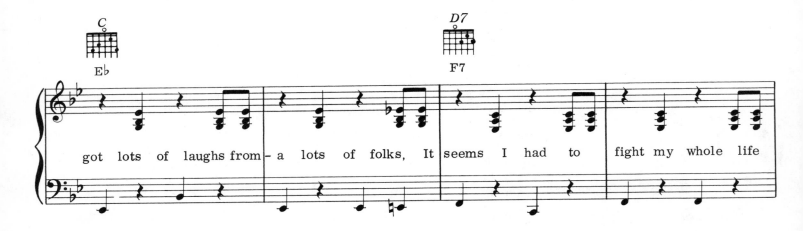

got lots of laughs from-a lots of folks, It seems I had to fight my whole life

through. Some gal would giggle and I'd get red, And

some guy would laugh and I'd bust his head; I tell you, life ain't easy for a boy named

For repeats

Last time

Sue.

3. (Well,) I grew up quick and I grew up mean, My fist got hard and my wits got keen,
Roamed from town to town to hide my shame. But I made me a vow to the moon and stars:
I'd search the honky tonks and bars and kill that man that give me that awful name.

4. But it was Gatlinburg in mid-July and I had just hit town and my throat was dry,
I'd thought I'd stop and have myself a brew. At an old saloon on a street of mud
And at a table dealing stud sat the dirty, mangy dog that named me Sue.

5. Well, I knew that snake was my own sweet dad from a worn-out picture that my mother had,
And I knew that scar on his cheek and his evil eye. He was big and bent and gray and old,
And I looked at him and my blood ran cold, and I said "My name is Sue. How do you do.
Now you're gonna die." Yeah, that's what I told him.

6. Well, I hit him right between the eyes and he went down, but to my surprise he come up with a knife
And cut off a piece of my ear. But I busted a chair right across his teeth, And we crashed through
the wall and into the street, Kicking and a-gouging in the mud and the blood and the beer.

7. I tell you I've fought tougher men but I really can't remember when,
He kicked like a mule and he bit like a crocodile. I heard him laughin' and then I heard him cussin',
He went for his gun and I pulled mine first. He stood there looking at me and I saw him smile.

8. And he said, "Son, this world is rough and if a man's gonna make it, he's gotta be tough;
And I knew I wouldn't be there to help you along. So I give you that name and I said 'Goodbye;'
I knew you'd have to get tough or die. And it's that name that helped to make you strong."

9. "Yeah," he said, "Now you have just fought one helluva fight, and I know you hate me and you've
got the right to kill me now, and I wouldn't blame you if you do. But you ought to thank me
before I die for the gravel in your guts and the spit in your eye because I'm the _ _ _ _
that named you Sue."

Yeah, what could I do? What could I do?

10. I got all choked up and I threw down my gun. Called him a pa and he called me a son,
And I come away with a different point of view. And I think about him now and then.
Every time I tried, every time I win and if I ever have a son I think I am gonna name him
Bill or George — anything but Sue.

Can The Circle Be Unbroken

Adapted and Arranged by Dan Fox

Chug-A-Lug

Words and Music by Roger Miller

Moderately, with a beat

1. Grape wine in a ma - son jar, home made and
2. 4 H and F. F. A. on a field trip
3. Juke box and a saw - dust floor, some - thin' like I ain't

brought to school by a friend of mine af - ter class.
to the farm Me and a friend mine sneak off be - hind
seen be - fore. And I'm just go - in' on fif - teen,

Me and him and this oth - er fool de - cide that we'll drink
this big old barn where we un - cov - ered a cov - ered - up
but with the help of my fin - a - gl - in' un - cle I

Crazy

Moderately slow

Words and Music by Willie Nelson

Crying Time

Words and Music by Buck Owens

Dang Me

Words and Music by Roger Miller

wom - an sit - tin' home_____ with a month old_____ child._____
lack_____ four - teen dol - lars hav - in' twen - ty sev - en cents.
pap - py was a pis - tol, I'm a son - of - a - gun._____

Chorus

Dang me, dang me, they ought-ta take a rope and hang me

high from the high - est tree, Wom - an, would you weep for me!

After repeats
D. S. al Coda

Coda

Detroit City

Words and Music by Danny Dill and Mel Tillis

Moderately

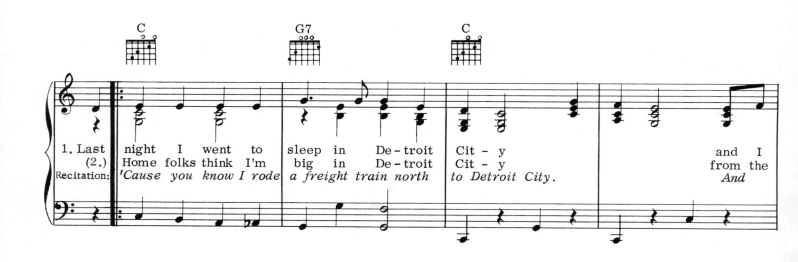

1. Last night I went to sleep in De-troit Cit - y
(2.) Home folks think I'm big in De-troit Cit - y
Recitation: 'Cause you know I rode a freight train north to Detroit City.

and I
from the
And

dreamed a - bout the cot - ton fields and home;
let - ters that I write they think I'm fine.
after all these years I find I've just been wasting my time,

I
But by
So I

Don't It Make My Brown Eyes Blue

Words and Music by Richard Leigh

I did-n't mean to treat you bad,_____ did-n't know just

what I had,___ But, hon-ey, now I do___ and

don't it make my brown eyes, don't it make my brown eyes,

don't it make my brown eyes blue. And

Repeat and fade

Do You Know
You Are My Sunshine

In a bright country 2 (♩ = 1 beat)

Words and Music by Don Reid and Harold Reid

Chorus

42

search-ing   ev-'ry crowd____   for her   face.____   She was
know____ just____ what____ I'm gon-na

say:____   "Do you   know,   Do you know____ you are my

sun   -   shine?   Do you know____   what your   smile____ did to

me?____   Do you   know,   Do you know____ you are____ my
Do you know   'You Are   My

Dreams Of The Everyday Housewife

Words and Music by Chris Gantry

46

saw her this way? _____
with-ered with age; _____

She holds up her a-pron in
She clos-es her eyes, _____ and

lit-tle girl fash-ion, as
touch-es the house-dress that ____

some-thing comes in-to her mind; _____
sud-den-ly dis-ap-pears; _____

Then
And

slow-ly starts danc-ing, re-
just for the mo-ment she's

mem-b'ring her girl-hood and
wear-ing the gown _____ that

all of the
broke all their

boys she had wait-ing in line; _____
minds ___ back so man-y years; _____

Ah;

Chorus

Such are the dreams of the ev - 'ry - day house-wife you see ev - 'ry-

where, an - y - time of the day;_____ Like the ev - 'ry - day

house - wife who gave up the good life for me._____

1.   2.

2. The

Easy Loving

Words and Music by Freddie Hart

ev-'ry day's__ Thanks - giv - ing,_____ To count all the bless - ings I would -n't know__ where to start. Ev -'ry time_____ I look you o - ver,__ So real to life it seems, Up - on your__ pret - ty shoul - ders_____ There's a

pair of ____ an - gel wings. ____ Eas - y

lov - ing, ____ see - ing's be - liev - ing, ____

Life ____ with you's like liv - ing in a beau - ti - ful

1. dream.

2. dream. ____

England Swings

Words and Music by Roger Miller

Lyrics:

En-ge-land swings like a pen-du-lum do, Bob-bies on bi-cy-cles two by two,

West-min-ster Ab-bey, the tower of Big Ben,— the ros-y red cheeks of the lit-tle chil-dren.

1. Now if you huff and puff and you
2. ___ Ma-ma's old pa-ja-mas and your

fin-'lly save e-nough mon-ey / up to take your fam - i - ly / on a trip a-cross the sea,___
pa-pa's mus - tache,_____ / Fall-in' out the win-dow sill, / fro-lic in the grass,_____

_____ Take a tip be-fore you / take your trip, let me tell you / where to go, Go to
Tryin' to mock the way they talk___ / but with all in vain,_____ /

1. F

2. F

D. S. al Coda

En - ge-land.___ Oh, / Gap-in' at the dap-per men with / der-by hats and canes.

Coda F

Repeat and fade

Whistle (8va higher on each repeat)_____
mp - p

Every Time Two Fools Collide

Words and Music by Jeff Tweel and Jan Dyer

*Guitarists tune 6th string to D.

in ev - 'ry-thing____ we do? And how long____ can we keep right and wrong____ so cut and dried?____ And who picks up the piec - es____ ev-'ry time_ two fools_ col - lide? We can save our love, we still have the

Everything Is Beautiful

Words and Music by Ray Stevens

59

free.___   For ev - e - ry hour   that pass-es   by___
in.___   We gon-na get it all to - geth-er now,___

you know the world gets a   lit-tle bit   old - er.   It's time   to   re - a - lize
and ev - 'ry-thing gon-na work out___   fine.___   Just take a lit-tle time___ to

              that beau - ty   lies   in the   eyes___   of the be-
look on the good side   my friend   And straight-en it out   in   your___

hold - er.___   And ev-'ry-thing is
mind.___   And ev-'ry-thing is

D. S. 𝄋
Last time to Coda

Coda

Flyin' Home To Nashville

Words and Music by Bill and Taffy Danoff

61

au - to - mo - tive hall ___ of fame ___ all framed in or - ange and
names on paint - ed bill - boards like ___ the cred - its flash - in' by ___
best of all ___ is make - be - lieve ___ and the worst of dreams come true

grey
Slip - pin' in and out ___ of fo - cus like ___ the
So I'll say so long ___ to Hol - ly - wood And the

And the cam - 'ra slow - ly pans ___ a - cross ___ the

air - port in L.
smog in both my
rest is up to

A.
eyes.
you.

We're all

Chorus

sing - ers in a choir, ___ we're all ___ play - ers in a play,

mf

62

The Fiddlers Of Ophir Creek

Words and Music by Pat and Victoria Garvey

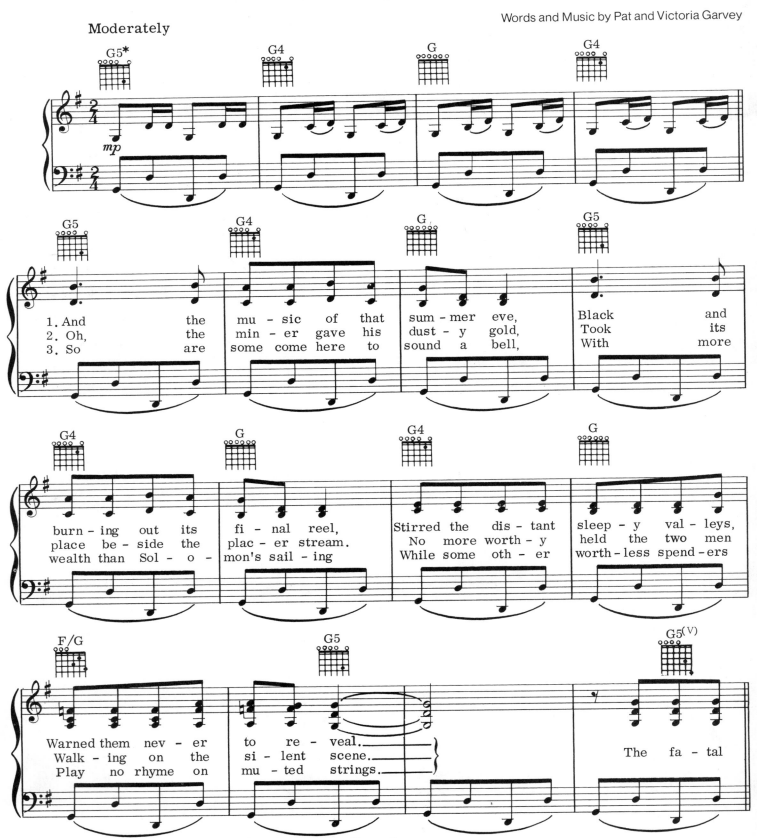

* Important note to guitarists: In this song the guitar is in G (or Vestapol)
tuning: 6th string = D, 5th = G, 4th, 3rd, and 2nd strings unchanged,
1st string = D. The chord diagrams are for guitar in this tuning.

Flowers On The Wall

Words and Music by Lew DeWitt

Note: *This song was recorded ½ step higher in B major. Pianists who wish to play with the record may mentally change the key signature to 5 sharps. Guitarists can capo up 4 instead of 3 frets.*

con-science, I guess.___ If
slow this swing-er down.___ So
cus-tomed to this light.___ And

in your shoes___ I would-n't wor-ry none,___ While
thought to me,___ I'm real-ly do-in' fine,___ And
not ac-cus-tomed to this hard con-crete,___ So

you 'n' your___ friends___ are wor - ryin' 'bout me I'm
you___ can___ al - ways find___ me here, I'm
I___ must___ go___ back to___ my room and

hav - in' lots of fun:
hav - in' quite a time:___}
make my day com - plete:___}   Count - in'

flow - ers on the wall that don't both - er me at all,

Play - in' sol - i - taire till

dawn with a deck of fif - ty one,

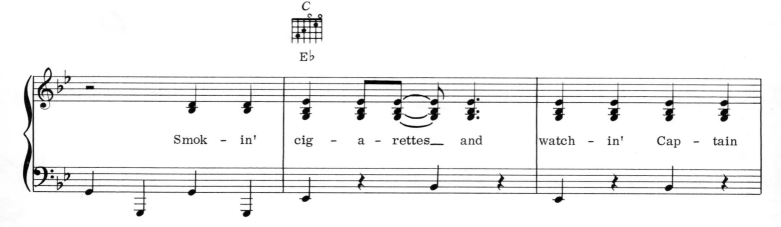

Smok - in' cig - a - rettes and watch - in' Cap - tain

Kan - ga - roo,___ Now don't_ tell me ___ I've noth-in' to

1. 2.
do.___ 2. Last
3. It's

3.
do,___ Don't tell

me ___ I've noth - in' to do.___

Don't tell me___ I've noth-in' to do.___

Folsom Prison Blues

Words and Music by Johnny Cash

Moderately (not too slow)

mf

Chorus

1. I hear the train a - com - in'; it's roll - in' 'round the bend, And
(2. When) I was just a ba - by my ma - ma told me, "Son, ____ And

I ain't seen the sun - shine since I don't know when. I'm
al - ways be a good boy; since don't ever play with guns. But I

stuck at Fol - som Pris - on and time keeps drag - gin'
shot a man in Re - no just ____ to watch him

3. I bet there's rich folks eatin' in a fancy dining car.
   They're prob'ly drinkin' coffee and smokin' big cigars,
   But I know I had it comin', I know I can't be free,
   But those people keep a-movin', and that's what tortures me.

4. Well, if they freed me from this prison, if that railroad train was mine,
   I bet I'd move on over a little farther down the line,
   Far from Folsom Prison, that's where I want to stay,
   And I'd let that lonesome whistle blow my blues away.

Funny How Time Slips Away

Words and Music by Willie Nelson

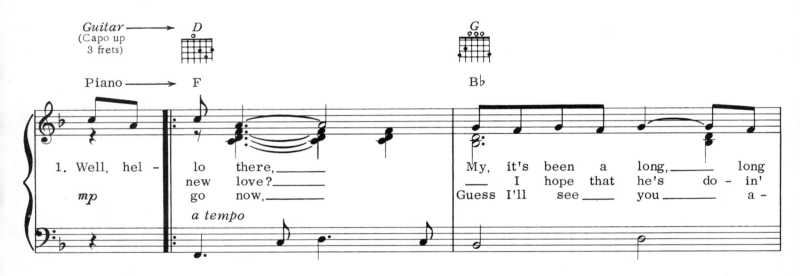

73

Gentle On My Mind

Words and Music by John Hartford

keeps you in the back roads by the riv-ers of my mem -'ry, That

keeps you ev - er gen-tle on my mind.

For additional verses

(It's not)

Final ending

2. It's not clinging to the rocks and ivy planted on their columns now that binds me
   Or something that somebody said because they thought we fit together walkin'.
   It's just knowing that the world will not be cursing or forgiving when I walk along
   Some railroad track and find
   That you're moving on the backroads by the rivers of my memory and for hours
   You're just gentle on my mind.

3. Though the wheat fields and the clothes lines and junkyards and the highways
   Come between us
   And some other woman crying to her mother 'cause she turned and I was gone.
   I still run in silence, tears of joy might stain my face and summer sun might
   Burn me 'til I'm blind
   But not to where I cannot see you walkin' on the backroads by the rivers flowing
   Gentle on my mind.

4. I dip my cup of soup back from the gurglin' cracklin' caldron in some train yard
   My beard a rough'ning coal pile and a dirty hat pulled low across my face.
   Through cupped hands 'round a tin can I pretend I hold you to my breast and find
   That you're waving from the backroads by the rivers of my memory ever smilin'
   Ever gentle on my mind.

76

Give Me Back
My Cool, Clean Water

Words and Music by Rick Shaw and Dick Clark

Moderately, in 2 (♩ = 1 beat)

1. Smoke stacks belch-ing clouds of thick black smoke in-to the sky,

Cit-ies pump-ing filth in-to the riv-ers run-ning by,

High-ways lined with lit-ter, rust-y beer cans ev-'ry-where,

Guitarists: tune 6th string to D.

Tell me, broth-er, don't you e-ven care?_____

2. Off-shore oil wells black-en miles_ of beach-es_ with_ their slime, And
gen-'rals who would dump their poi - son gas - es in__ the sea And
be our chil-dren's leg - a - cy__ will they wake to__ sum-mer's dream? Will they

D. D. T.__ is knock-ing na-ture's rea-son out of rhyme,_____ How
men who tam - per blind-ly with_the world e - col-o-gy,_____ The
know the joy__ of walk-ing by__ a crys-tal moun-tain stream?__ Will they

long can we stand si - lent and pre-tend we just don't see When
ra - ven flies a - cross the sun_____ his cry - in' fills the day Or
sail up - on the winds and wa - ters__ flow-in' fresh and fair When

Moth-er Na-ture cries to you and me:___
Lis-ten, peo-ple, hear me when I say:___
will they be the vic-tims of a world___ that did not care?

Chorus

Give me back my cool, clean wa-ter,___

Give me back my clear blue sky,___

Give me back my spark-lin'___ sea-shore,___ Fish that

swim and birds that fly.___
3. There are fly.___
4. What will

Goodbye, My Sweet Johnny

Words and Music by Jim Friedman and Tennise Broeck

Moderately, in 2 (𝅗𝅥 = 1 beat)

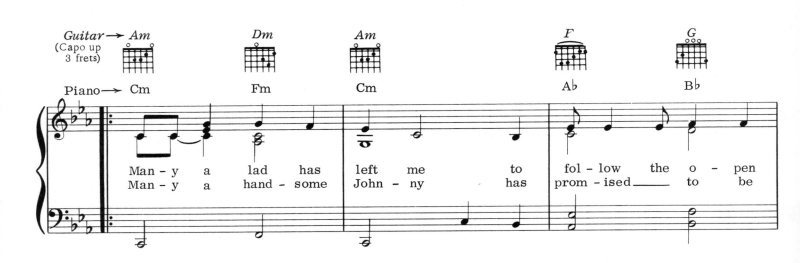

Man - y a lad has left me to fol - low the o - pen
Man - y a hand - some John - ny has prom - ised___ to be

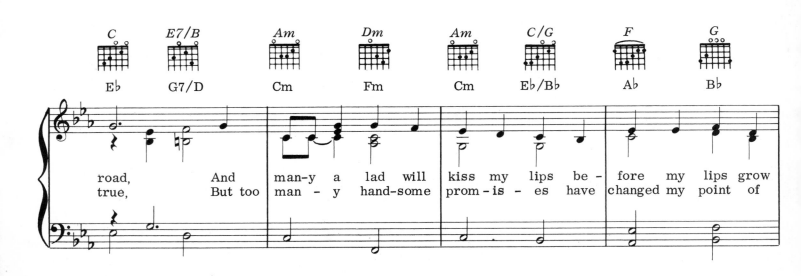

road, And man-y a lad will kiss my lips be - fore my lips grow
true, But too man - y hand-some prom - is - es have changed my point of

Gotta Travel On

Words and Music by Paul Clayton

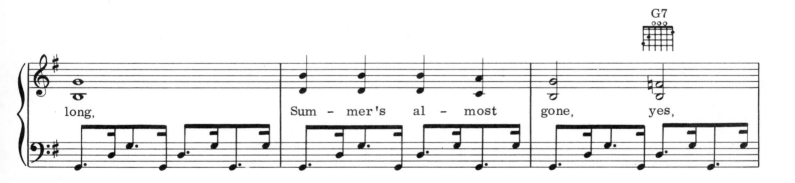

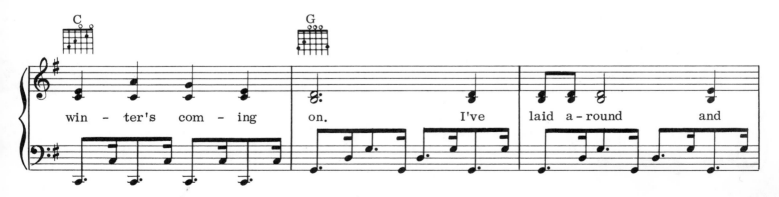

played a-round   this old town too   long   And I

C   D7   *To Coda* ⊕ G
                                           (last time)

feel like I've   got - ta tra - vel   on. _____

Verse G

1. Pop-pa writes   to   John - ny,   but   John - ny   can't   come
2. High_ sher - iff   and   po - lice   rid - ing   af - ter
3. Want to see   my   hon - ey,   want   to   see   her

                                                                        G7

home.   John - ny   can't   come   home,   no,
me,   Rid - ing   af - ter   me,   yes,
bad,   Want   to   see   her   bad,   oh,

Gospel Changes

Words and Music by Jack Williams

Slowly, but with a steady beat

The

D* **A** **Bm**
Prod-i-gal Son, he'd been a-way a while, he was
Je-sus, He did not doubt His gifts, though He
Je-ru-salem, I see you stand-ing high, but if you

G **A** **D**
work-ing his way back home now o-ver man-y a rag-ged mile. When he
knew that He had not long to live. He
lose your sal-va-tion there'll be no tears left to cry. Now

G **Em** **D** **F#m/C#** **Bm**
fi-nal-ly crossed the riv-er and his fa-ther saw him near, there was a
took care of the bus-'ness of teachin' us how to fly, then He
some men wor-ship a Gold-en Calf, while others are bought and sold, and if we

* Guitarists: Tune lowest string to D.

joy - ful sound___ for all the world__ to hear;___ } I
bowed His head___ and laid__ down__ to die.___ }
live like that,___ broth - er we pay___ the toll.___ }

lis-tened to what__ the Good__ Book said and it made good sense to me,___ talk-in' 'bout

reap-in' what you're sow-in'___ peo-ple try-in' to be free.__ Now we've got new names and fa - ces,

this time a - round,__ Gos-pel chang-es, Lord,__ still go-in' down.___

Grandma's Feather Bed

Words and Music by Jim Connor

Moderately fast

When I was a lit-tle bit-ty boy just up off — a
Af-ter supper we'd sit a-round the fire, the old folks'd spit — and

floor,   We used to go down to Grand-ma's house
chew,   Pa would talk a-bout the farm and the war, and

ev - 'ry month-end or so, We'd have chick-en pie and coun-try ham__ 'n'
Gran-ny'd sing a bal-lad or two. I'd sit and listen and watch the fire__ till the

home - made but-ter on the bread, But the best darn thing a-bout
cob - webs filled my head, Next thing I'd know I'd

Grand - ma's house was her great big__ feath-er bed.}
wake up in the morn-in' in the mid-dle of the old feath-er bed.} It was

Chorus

nine feet tall and six feet wide, soft as a down-y chick. It was

Well, I

love my Ma, I love my Pa,__ I love Gran-ny and Grand-pa too, I been

fish-in' with my un-cle, I ras-sled with my cou-sin, I e-ven kissed__ Aunt

Lou ooo! But if I ev-er had__ to make a choice, I guess it ought-a be

said   That I'd trade 'em all __ plus the gal down the road   for Grand-ma's __ feath - er

bed.   I'd trade 'em all __ plus the gal down the road...   It was

D.S. al Coda 𝄋

Coda ⊕

bed.   We did-n't get much sleep but we   had a lot of fun   on   Grand-ma's __ feath - er

bed.

92

Heartaches By The Number

Words and Music by Harlan Howard

Chorus

94

heart - aches by the num - ber, _____ A love that I can't win, But the day that I stop count - ing, That's the

1.
day my world will end. _____

2. E7
F7
day my world will end. _____
A
Bb

Green,Green Grass Of Home

Words and Music by Curly Putman

Chorus

Harper Valley PTA

Words and Music by Tom T. Hall

(*Recitation*):
2. The note said, Mrs. Johnson, you're wearing your dresses way too high—
It's reported you've been drinking and a-runnin' 'round with men and going wild.
We don't believe you ought to be a-bringing up your little girl this way—
It was signed by the secretary, Harper Valley P-T.A.

3. Well, it happened that the P-T.A. was gonna meet that very afternoon—
They were sure surprised when Mrs. Johnson wore her mini-skirt into the room.
As she walked up to the blackboard, I still recall the words she had to say.
She said, "I'd like to address this meeting of the Harper Valley P.T.A.

4. Well, there's Bobby Taylor sittin' there and seven times he's asked me for a date.
Mrs. Taylor sure seems to use a lot of ice whenever he's away.
And Mr. Baker, can you tell us why your secretary had to leave this town?
And shouldn't widow Jones be told to keep her window shades all pulled completely down?

5. Well, Mr. Harper couldn't be here 'cause he stayed too long at Kelly's bar again.
And if you smell Shirley Thompson's breath, you'll find she's had a little nip of gin.
Then you have the nerve to tell me you think that as a mother I'm not fit.
Well, this is just a little Peyton Place and you're all Harper Valley hypocrites.
No, I wouldn't put you on, because it really did, it happened just this way,
The day my mama socked it to the Harper Valley P-T.A.

Heartbreak Hotel

Words and Music by Mae Boren Axton, Tommy Durden and Elvis Presley

In a steady four

1. Since my ba - by left me, ___ found a new place to dwell
4. If your ba - by leaves you and you have___ a tale to tell,

Down at the end of Lone - ly Street at Heart-break Ho - tel.___
Just take a walk down Lone - ly Street to Heart-break Ho - tel.___

I get so lone - ly, ba-by, I get so lone - ly, I get so

Hello Walls

Words and Music by Willie Nelson

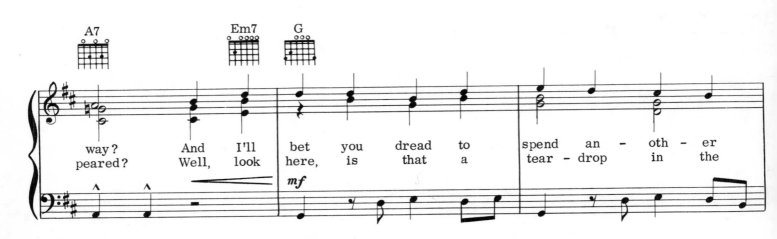

ceil-ing,_____ I'm gon-na stare at you a while. You know I

can't sleep, So won't you bear with me a while? We must

all pull to-geth - er or else I'll lose my mind, 'Cause I've got a

feel-in' she'll be gone a long, long time._____

Help Me Make It Through The Night

Words and Music by Kris Kristofferson

Honey

Words and Music by Bobby Russell

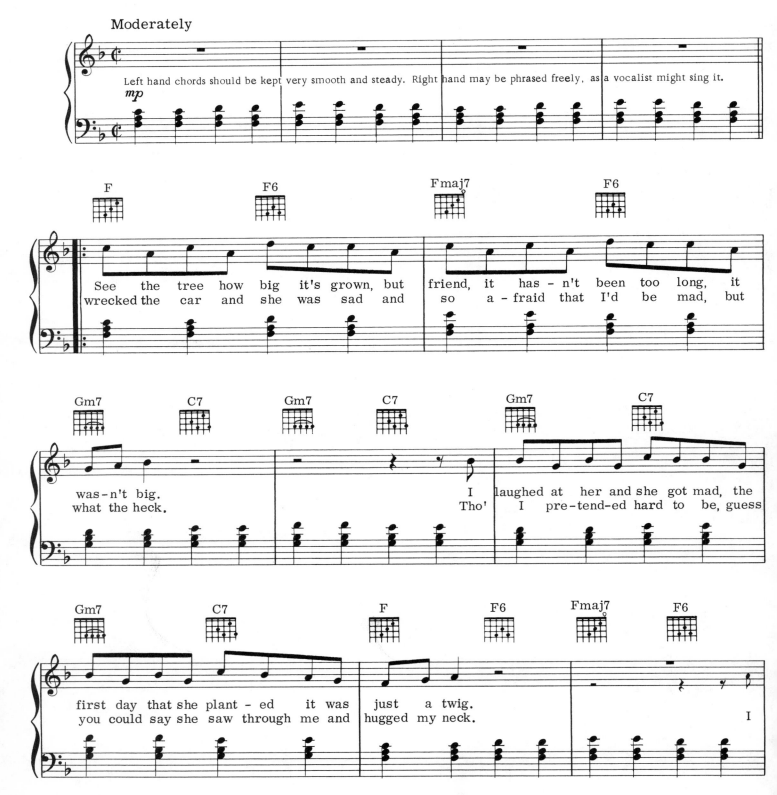

108

loved her so.
an-gels came.

Now
I sur-prised her with a pup-py;
all I have is mem-o-ries of

kept me up all Christ-mas eve two years a-go.
Hon-ey, and I wake up nights and call her name.

And

it would sure em-bar-rass her when
Now my life's an emp-ty stage where

I came home from work-ing late 'cause
Hon-ey lived and Hon-ey played and

I would know
love grew up.

That she'd been sit-tin' there and cry-in'
A small cloud pass-es o-ver-head and

Honey Be There

Words and Music by Dan Wheetman

ey,   And I caught a ride down High-way   One that was
coast - line,   The on - ly thing that makes it right_____ is
long,   The on - ly thing that makes it right_____ is

go - in'   to L.   A.   Just twelve more   hours___   and if
sea and   sun-shine,   A man that's shack-led   dies a
sing -in' a good   song,   I try   not to think a - bout what's

ev - 'ry-thing's all   right   I'll be   roll - in' in ___ your
lone - ly death in - side.   I'm___ born a - gain___ each
wrong   and what is   right.   And I'll be   roll - in' in ___ your

(Last time, repeat Chorus and fade)

lov - in'   arms___ to - night.____
time   I   catch___ a   ride.
lov - in'   arms___ to - night.____

113

Hound Dog

Words and Music by Jerry Leiber and Mike Stoller

I Can't Help But Wonder
(Where I'm Bound)

Words and Music by Tom Paxton

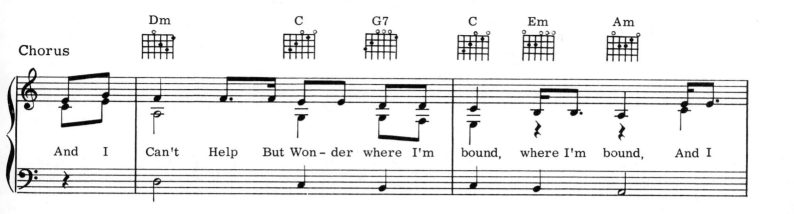

Chorus

And I | Can't Help But Won-der where I'm | bound, where I'm bound, And I

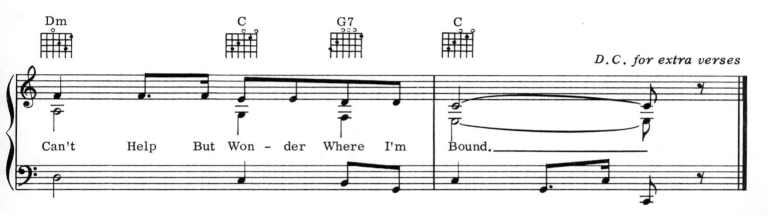

D.C. *for extra verses*

Can't Help But Won - der Where I'm | Bound._____

Additional   Verses

2. I have been around this land
   Just a-doin' the best I can
   Tryin' to find what I was meant to do.
   And the faces that I see
   Are as worried as can be
   And it looks like they are wonderin' too.
   (Chorus)

3. I had a little gal one time
   She had lips like sherry wine
   And she loved me till my head went plumb insane
   But I was too blind to see
   She was driftin' away from me
   And one day she left on the morning train.
   (Chorus)

4. I've got a buddy from home
   But he started out to roam
   And I hear he's out by Frisco Bay
   And sometimes when I've had a few
   His voice comes singin' through
   And I'm goin' out to see him some old day
   (Chorus)

5. If you see me passing by
   And you sit and wonder why
   And you wish that you were a rambler, too,
   Nail your shoes to the kitchen floor
   Lace 'em up and bar the door
   Thank your stars for the roof that's over you.
   (Chorus)

I Fall To Pieces

Words and Music by Hank Cochran and Harlan Howard

nev - er kissed,_____ You want me to for - get, pre-tend we've
else to love,_____ Some - one who'll love me, too, the way you

nev - er met,_____ And I've tried_____ and I've tried, but I
used to do,_____ But each time_____ I go out with_

have - n't yet,_____ You walk by and I fall to
some - one new,_____ You walk by and and I fall to

1.
piec - es._____

2.
piec - es.
rall.

Hitch-Hiker

Words and Music by Dick Reicheg and Eric Weissberg

numb from stick - in' out my thumb, But if
song if from you just take me a - long,

I can just keep mov - in' then__ I'll be sat - is - fied.
you don't like my sing - in' we can just talk pol - i - tics. Oh, I'm a

Chorus

Hitch - hik - er, I'm a boy with - out a

home__ a suit - case and my old gui - tar are the

only things I own, and though I've tried to set-tle

down _____ in man-y a cit-y and town, _____ the

on-ly time I'm hap-py is when I'm ram-blin'

'round. _____ You might 'round. _____

I Never Will Marry

New Words and New Music by Fred Hellerman

2. Well, the   life.

D. S. al Coda 𝄋

Coda ⊕

life.

slower- - - - - - - - - - - - -

I Walk The Line

Words and Music by Johnny Cash

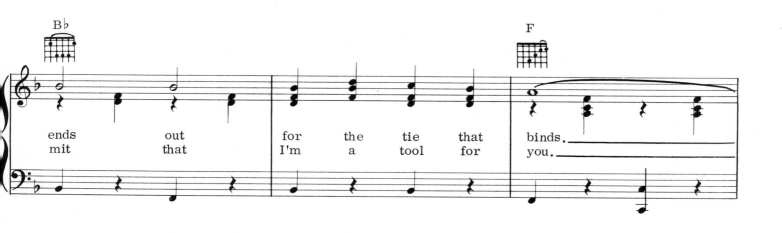

ends out for the tie that binds._____
mit that I'm a tool for you._____

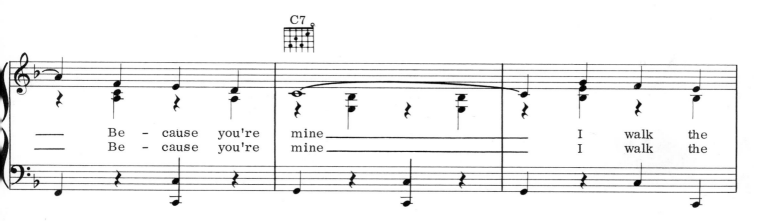

_____ Be - cause you're mine_____ I walk the
_____ Be - cause you're mine_____ I walk the

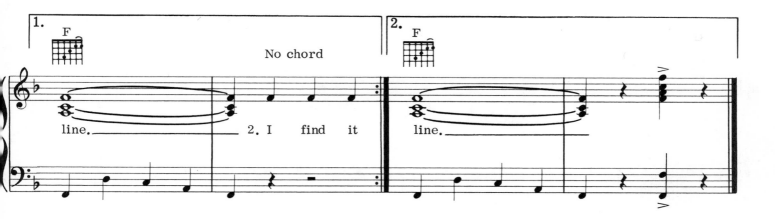

line._____ 2. I find it
line._____

3. As sure as night is dark and day is light,
   I keep you on my mind both day and night.
   And happiness I've known proves that it's right.
   Because you're mine I walk the line.

4. You've got a way to keep me on your side.
   You give me cause for love that I can't hide.
   For you I know I'd even try to turn the tide.
   Because you're mine I walk the line.

5. I keep a close watch on this heart of mine.
   I keep my eyes wide open all the time.
   I keep the ends out for the tie that binds.
   Because you're mine I walk the line.

I Was There

Words and Music by Don Reid

prom I must con - fess____ When the last dance was danced I was
all____ have our breaks____ When she broke her first heart I was

1. there. 2. When I

2. there. 3. When she

walked down the aisle____ I was there;
last time we met____ he was there,

When she
And what-

took the vows to al-ways love and care.____
ev - er he thinks____ I don't care.____

With
____

129

I Will Always Love You

Words and Music by Dolly Parton

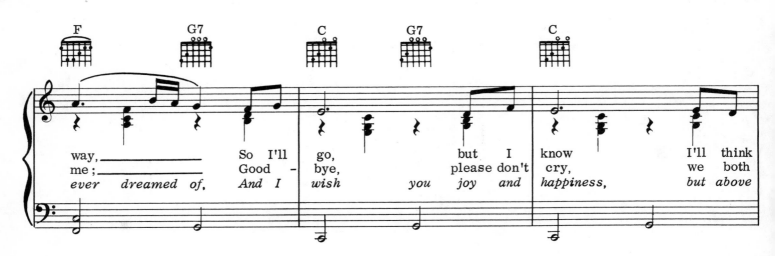

I'll Go To My Grave Loving You

Words and Music by Don Reid

go ___ (I'll go) to my grave ___ (to my grave) lov - in'

you, (lov - in' you.) lov - in' you. Oh, to take ___

___ his place for - ev - er, ___ there's noth - ing ___ I would-n't give.

___ I'd prove ___ to you dai - ly ___

136

I'm Just A Country Boy

Words and Music by Fred Hellerman and Marshall Barer

Chorus

I'm just a coun - try boy___ Mon - ey have I none, But I've got sil - ver in the stars And gold in the morn - ing sun, And gold in the morn - ing sun.

2. I'm
3. I

sun.

I'm Leaving It (All) Up To You

Words and Music by Don Harris and Dewey Terry, Jr.

Slow Rock tempo

It Wasn't God Who Made Honky Tonk Angels

Moderately

Words and Music by J. D. Miller

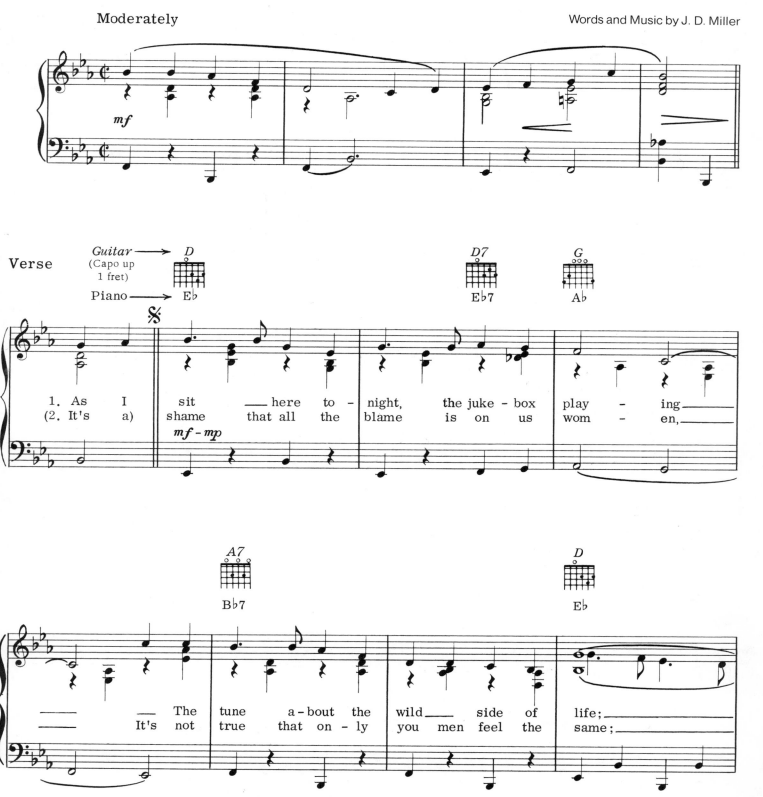

Verse

1. As I sit ___ here to - night, the juke - box play - ing ___
(2. It's a) shame that all the blame is on us wom - en, ___

___ The tune a-bout the wild ___ side of life; ___
___ It's not true that on - ly you men feel the same; ___

As I lis-ten to the words_____ you are say - ing,_____
From the start most ev-'ry heart that's ev - er bro - ken,_____

It brings mem-'ries when I was a trust-ing wife._____
Was be - cause there al-ways was a man to blame._____

Chorus

It was - n't God who made honk - y tonk

an - gels,_____ As you said in the

144

145

Jimmy Brown The Newsboy

Moderately

Words and Music by A. P. Carter

Jolene

Words and Music by Dolly Parton

Last time
to Coda

Jo - lene, Jo - lene, Jo - lene, Jo - lene

please don't take him {just be - cause } even though } you

can. Your (He)

beau - ty is be- yond com - pare, with
talks a - bout you in his sleep and there's
You could have your choice of men but

flam - ing locks of au - burn hair, with
noth - ing I can do to keep from
I could nev - er love a - gain

iv - 'ry skin and eyes of em - 'rald green
cry - ing when he calls your name, Jo - lene
He's the on - ly one for me, Jo - lene

Your smile is like a breath of spring, your
And I can eas - 'ly un - der - stand your how my
I had to have this talk with you, my

voice is soft like sum - mer rain, and
you could eas - 'ly take my man, but you
hap - pi - ness de - pends on you and what -

I can - not com - pete with you,
don't know what he means to me,
ev - er you de - cide to do,

King Of The Road

Words and Music by Roger Miller

Moderately, with a bounce

Little Green Apples

Words and Music by Bobby Russell

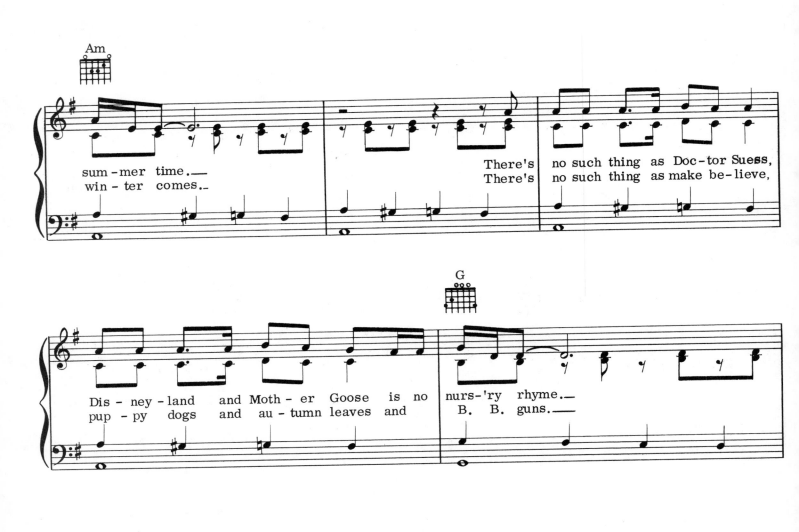

sum - mer time.— / win - ter comes.—

There's no such thing as Doc - tor Suess,
There's no such thing as make be - lieve,

Dis - ney - land and Moth - er Goose is no nurs - 'ry rhyme.—
pup - py dogs and au - tumn leaves and B. B. guns.—

God did - n't make lit - tle green ap - ples and it don't rain in In - dian - ap - 'lis in the

sum - mer - time,—

And when my - self is feel - in' low I

The Long Black Veil

Words and Music by Marijohn Wilkin and Danny Dill

159

Love Me Tender

Words and Music by Elvis Presley and Vera Matson

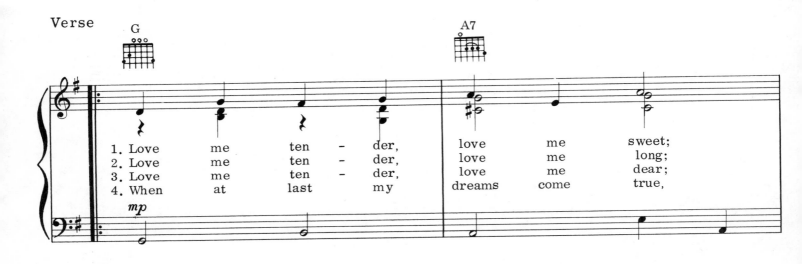

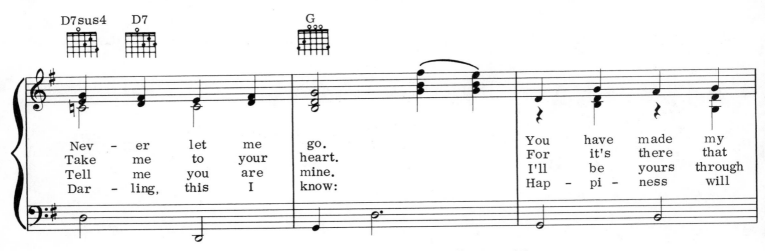

life com - plete, And I love you so.
I be - long, And we'll nev - er part.
all the years, Till the end of time.
fol - low you Ev - 'ry - where you go.

Chorus

Love me ten - der, love me true, All my dreams ful -

fill. For, my dar - lin', I love you,

1. 2. 3.

And I al - ways will.

4.

And I al - ways will.

161

Lou'siana Young

Words and Music by Ron Shaw

al - most smell the cat - fish
some folks say I've made it, But I fry - in' in the won - der in what they

pan, I And it takes me back to the time when I was
mean, I got a fan - cy house and a fan - cy car and my

young in Lou' - si - anne.
fin - ger - nails are clean. I wan - na be

Lou' - si - an - a, Lou' - si - an - a young a-

163

E7

Driv - in' down the road from Maine to Tex - as,

E7   Am

Sell - in' things I'd nev - er buy my - self,

D7   G

Mon-ey ain't bad but the ly - in' don't come eas - y,   And that

D7   G7

bare - foot kid re - minds me of my young - er self. I wan-na be

166

Love Of The Common People

Words and Music by John Hurley and Ronnie Wilkins

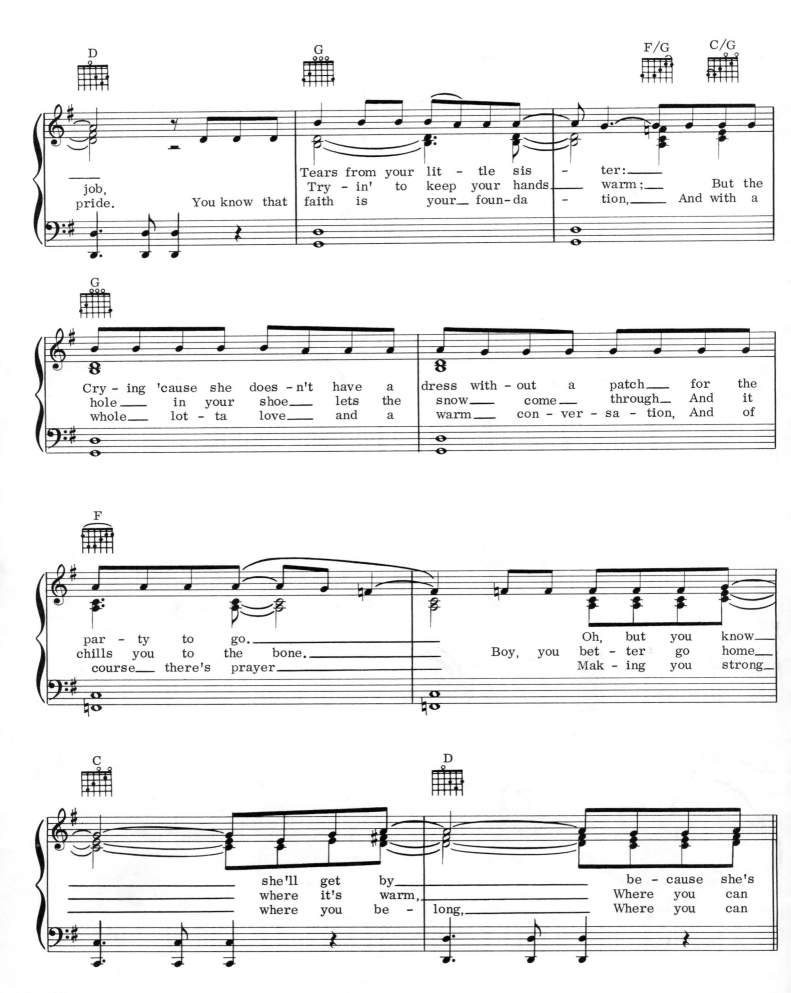

Love Or Something Like It

Words and Music by Kenny Rogers and Steve Glassmeyer

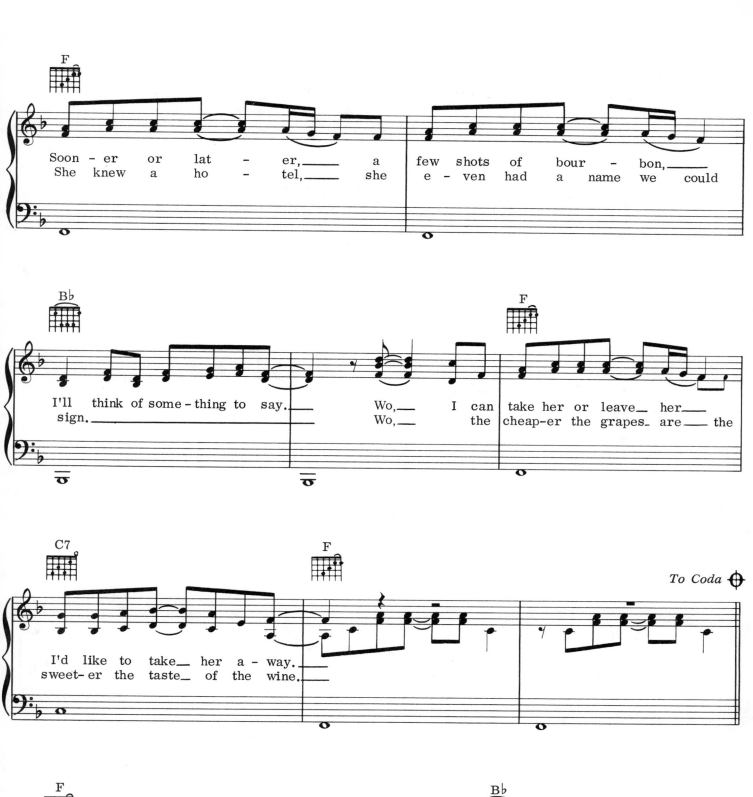

Soon - er or lat - er,_____ a few shots of bour - bon,_____
She knew a ho - tel,_____ she e - ven had a name we could

I'll think of some - thing to say.____ Wo,____ I can take her or leave_ her.____
sign._____ Wo,____ the cheap-er the grapes_ are __ the

I'd like to take_ her a - way.____
sweet-er the taste_ of the wine.____

To Coda ⊕

Li-quor and mu - sic,_ A good com-bi - na - tion_ if you've got love_ on the brain.

174

Lucille

Words and Music by R. Bowling and H. Bynum

sat down___ and asked her her name.___
had a ___ strange look on his face.___

When the
The

drinks fin - 'ly hit___ her,___ she said, "I'm___ no a quit - ter,___ but I
big hands were cal - loused, he looked like___ a moun-tain,___ for a

fin - 'ly quit liv - ing___ on dreams.
min - ute I thought I___ was dead.

I'm
But

hun - gry___ for laugh - ter___ and here ev - er af - ter,___
he start - ed shak - ing,___ his big heart was break - ing,___

I'm
he

176

af - ter what-ev - er___ the oth-er__ life brings." In the

turned to the wom-an___ and said: You picked a

fine time to leave___ me, Lu - cille, with four hun - gry chil-

- dren and a crop in the field. I've had___ some

bad times,___ lived through___ some sad times,___ but this time_____ your

hurt - in' won't heal,

You picked a fine time_____ to

leave me, Lu - cille.

Af - ter_____ he left us___ I or - dered_ more_ whis - key,___ I

thought how_____ she made him look small. From the

lights of the bar - room to a rent-ed__ ho - tel__ room,_ we

walked with - out talk - ing_____ at all.

She was_ a beau - ty,_ but when she_ came_ to_ me,_ she

four hun - gry chil - dren and a crop in the field.

I've had____ some bad times,____ lived through____ some

sad times,____ but this time____ your hurt - in' won't heal,

Repeat and fade

You picked a fine time____ to leave me, Lu - cille.   You picked a

181

Make The World Go Away

Words and Music by Hank Cochran

Moderately slow, with a lilt

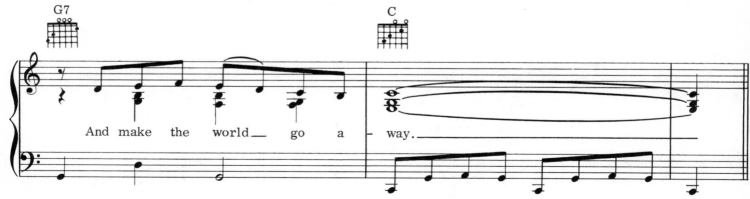

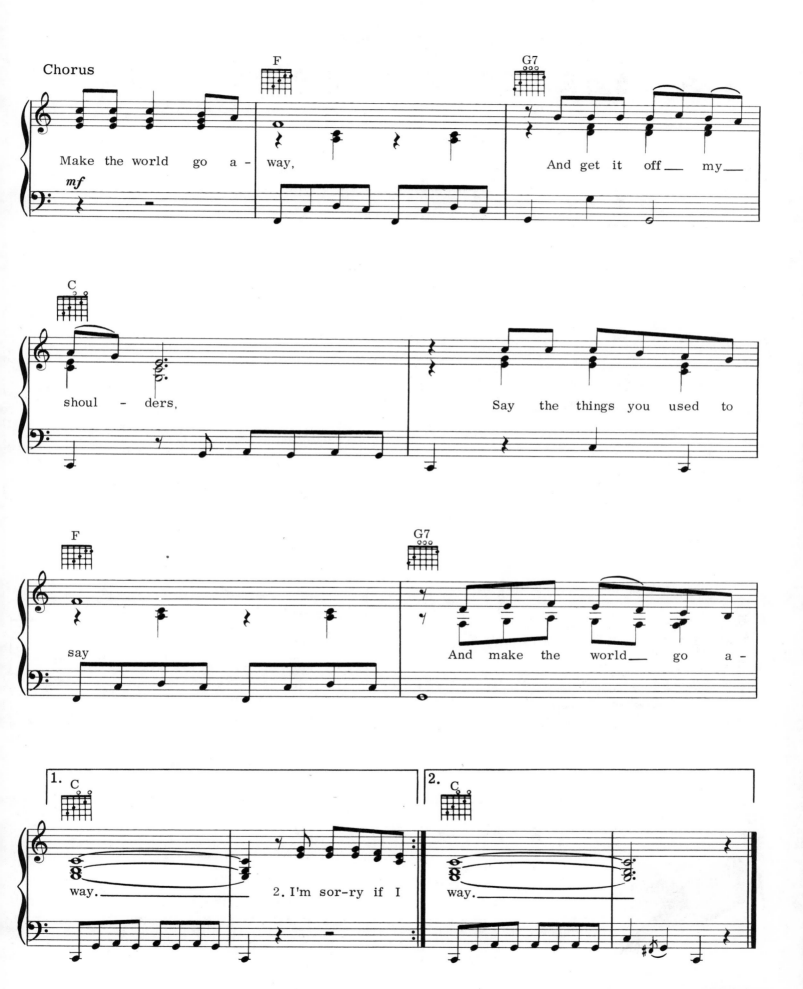

Mammas Don't Let Your Babies Grow Up To Be Cowboys

Words and Music by Ed Bruce and Patsy Bruce

Lone star belt buck-les__ and old fad-ed
Them that don't know him__ won't like him and

G / Bb

Le-vis and each night be-gins__ a new day.__ If you
them that do some-times won't know how__ to take him, He ain't

A7 / C7

don't un-der-stand him and he don't die__ young, he'll prob-'ly
wrong, he's just dif-f'rent but his pride__ won't__ let him do things to make

D / F   **A7 / C7**

just ride__ a - way.
you think__ he's right.

Chorus

Mam-mas, don't let your ba - bies grow up to be cow - boys, Don't let them pick gui - tars and drive them old trucks, Let them be doc - tors and law - yers and such.

186

Mam - mas,___ don't let your ba - bies grow up to be

cow - boys, 'cause they'll

nev - er___ stay home and they're al - ways a - lone___ e - ven___ with

After repeat
D. S. and fade

some - one they love.___

187

(Lying Here With)
Linda On My Mind

Moderately slow

Words and Music by Conway Twitty

To next strain

E7

side— her with Lin- da— on— my mind.

A

Yes, I

Fine

D

mind.—

rit.

A

A

know that I once loved her and I place— no one a- a-
loved you for a long time, but you're mar - ried to a

A7

bove— her,— And I nev- er thought— I'd ev - er set her
friend— of — mine,— And I try hard— to nev- er let it

D

Me And Bobby McGee

Words and Music by Kris Kristofferson and Fred Foster

poon out of____ my | dirt-y red ban- | dan-na | And was blow-in' sad_ while | Bob-by sang the
lin - as, Lord,_ I | let her slip a - | way | Look-in' for_ the | home I hope she'll

blues;_____ ___ With them wind-shield wip-ers | slap-pin' time and | Bob-by clap-pin'
find;_____ And I'd trade all of my to- | mor-rows for a | sin-gle yes-ter-

hands We fin-'ly | sang up ev-'ry | song that driv-er__ | knew,}
day, Hold-in' Bob-by's | bod - y next to__ | mine.}

Free-dom's just an-oth-er__ word for | noth-in'__ left to lose,__

mf

Mockin' Bird Hill

Words and Music by Vaughn Horton

Moderately fast country waltz

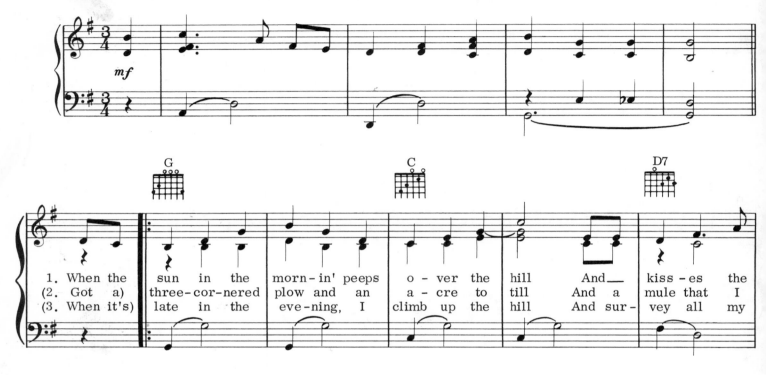

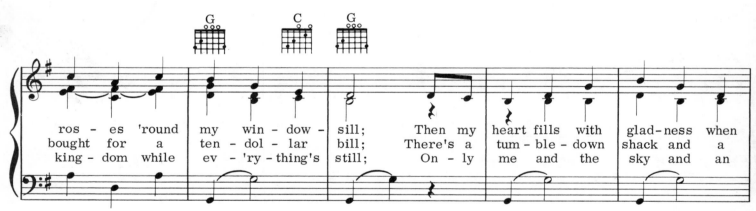

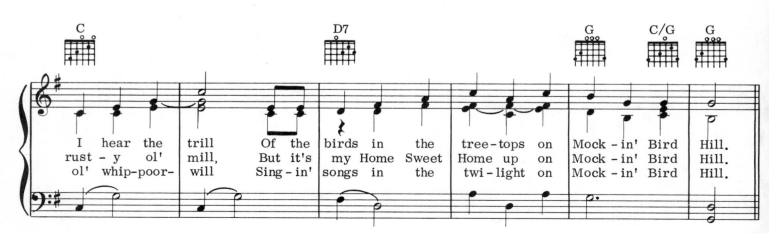

My Elusive Dreams

Words and Music by Curly Putman and Billy Sherrill

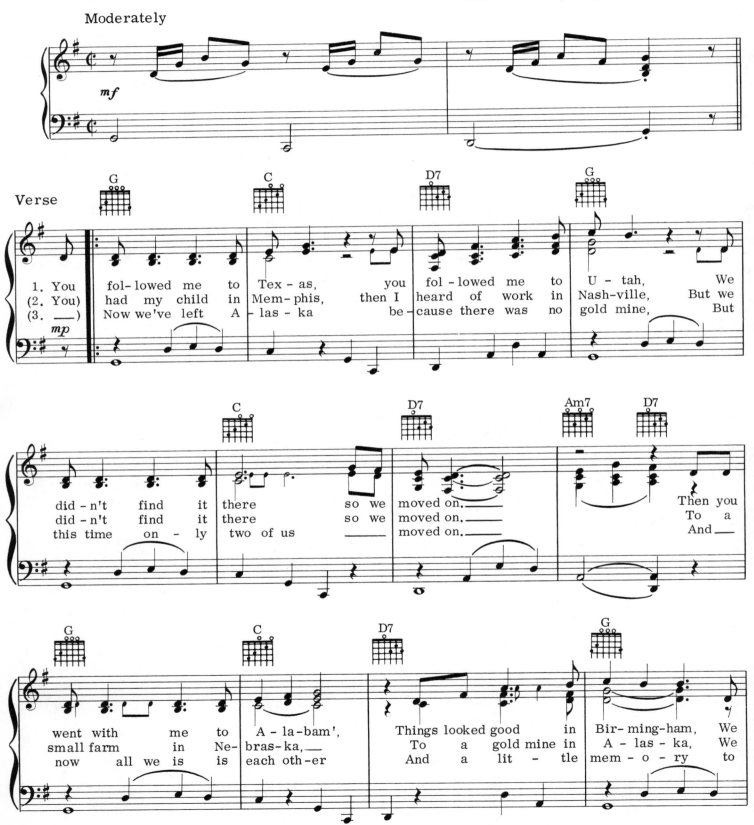

196

did – n't find it there so we moved on._____
did – n't find it there so we moved on._____
cling to and_____ still you won't let me go on a - lone.

Chorus

N. C.

I know you're tired of fol - low - ing my e - lu - sive

dreams and schemes,_____ For they're on - ly fleet - ing things,

1. 2.

my e - lu - sive dreams._____ 2. You dreams.
3._____

My Ramblin' Boy

Words and Music by Tom Paxton

Moderately

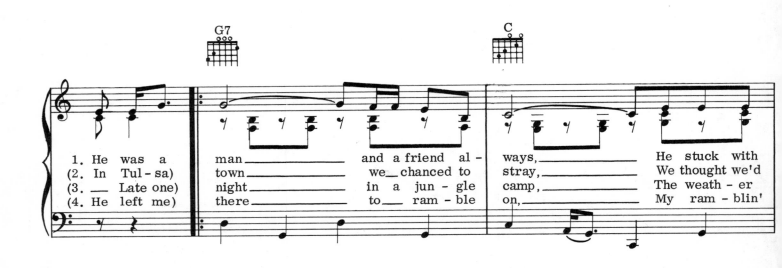

1. He was a man_____ and a friend al - ways,_____ He stuck with
(2. In Tul - sa) town_____ we_ chanced to stray,_____ We thought we'd
(3. __ Late one) night_____ in a jun - gle camp,_____ The weath - er
(4. He left me) there_____ to_ ram - ble on,_____ My ram - blin'

me_____ in the hard old days,_____ He nev - er cared_____ if I had no
try_____ to_ work one day._____ The boss said he_____ had_ room for
it_____ was_ cold and damp._____ He got the chills_____ and he got 'em
pal_____ is_ dead and gone._____ If when we die_____ we_ go some -

dough,_____ We ram-bled
one;_____ Says my old
bad,_____ They took the
where,_____ I'll bet you a

round_____ in the rain and
pal,_____ "We'd_ rath-er
on - ly_ friend I
dollar_____ he's_ ram-blin'

snow.
bum!"
had.
there.
} And here's to

you,_____ my ram-blin' boy,_____ May all your ram - blin' bring you

joy._____ And here's to you,_____ my ram-blin' boy,_____ May all your

ram - blin' bring you joy._____

2. In Tul-sa
3. _ Late one
4. He left me

joy._____

Okie From Muskogee

Words and Music by Merle Haggard and Roy Edward Burris

Ode To Billy Joe

Words and Music by Bobbie Gentry

eat,_____

And Ma-ma hol-lered at the back door, "Y'all re-

mem - ber to wipe your feet."_____

Then she

said, "I got some news this morn – in' from Choc-taw Ridge,_____

To - day_____ Bil - ly Joe Mc - Al - lis - ter jumped

off the Tal-la-hat-chee Bridge."

2. Papa said to Mama, as he passed around the black-eyed peas,
   "Well, Billy Joe never had a lick o' sense, pass the biscuits please,
   There's five more acres in the lower forty I've got to plow."
   And Mama said it was a shame about Billy Joe anyhow.
   Seems like nothin' ever comes to no good up on Choctaw Ridge,
   And now Billy Joe McAllister's jumped off the Tallahatchee Bridge.

3. Brother said he recollected when he and Tom and Billy Joe,
   Put a frog down my back at the Carroll County picture show,
   And wasn't I talkin' to him after church last Sunday night,
   I'll have another piece of apple pie, you know, it don't seem right.
   I saw him at the sawmill yesterday on Choctaw Ridge,
   And now you tell me Billy Joe's jumped off the Tallahatchee Bridge.

4. Mama said to me, "Child, what's happened to your appetite?
   I been cookin' all mornin' and you haven't touched a single bite,
   That nice young preacher Brother Taylor dropped by today,
   Said he'd be pleased to have dinner on Sunday, Oh, by the way,
   He said he saw a girl that looked a lot like you up on Choctaw Ridge,
   And she an' Billy Joe was throwin' somethin' off the Tallahatchee Bridge."

5. A year has come and gone since we heard the news 'bout Billy Joe,
   Brother married Becky Thompson, they bought a store in Tupelo,
   There was a virus goin' 'round, Papa caught it and died last spring,
   And now Mama doesn't seem to want to do much of anything.
   And me I spend a lot of time pickin' flowers up on Choctaw Ridge,
   And drop them into the muddy water off the Tallahatchee Bridge.

Oklahoma Hills

Moderately

Words and Music by Woody Guthrie and Jack Guthrie

page   of   life   has   turned   and   a   les -   son   I   have
oak   and   black - jack   trees   kiss   the   play -   ful   prai - rie
black   oil   rolls   and   flows   and   the   snow - white   cot - ton

learned,   Yet   I   feel   like   in   those
breeze,   In   those   Ok -   la -   ho -   ma
grows,   In   those   Ok -   la -   ho -   ma

hills   I   still   be -   long.
Hills   where   I   was   born.
Hills   where   I   was   born.

Chorus

Way   down   yon - der   in   the   In -   dian   na -   tion,

207

Paper Roses

Words and Music by Janice Torre and Fred Spielman

The Pill

Words and Music by Lorene Allen, Don McHan and T.D. Bayless

Moderately fast

bill,_____ I'm__ tear - in' down your brood - er house 'cause
Hill,_____ You've_ set this chick - en your last time, 'cause
deal,_____ And you can't af - ford to turn it down 'cause you

now I've got the pill.
now I've got the pill.
know I've got the pill.

(to repeat)
(to 2nd ending and Chorus 1)
(to 3rd ending and Chorus 2)

Chorus 1. This
Chorus 2. This

old ma - ter - ni - ty dress I've got____ is go - in' in the
in - cu - bat - or is o - ver used____ be - cause you kept it

gar - bage,_____ The clothes I'm wear - in' from now on ___ won't
filled,_____ The feel - ing good comes eas - y now___ ___

take up so much yard - age! _____ ___ ___ Min - i skirts and
since I've got the pill! _____

hot pants with a few lit - tle fan - cy frills, _____ Yeah, I'm
roost - ing time, to - night's too good to be real, _____ And ___

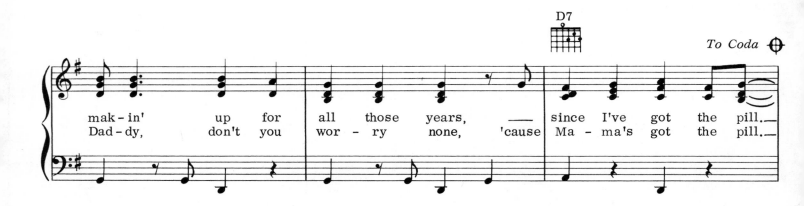

To Coda ⊕

mak - in' up for all those years, ___ since I've got the pill. _
Dad - dy, don't you all wor - ry none, 'cause Ma - ma's got the pill. _

D.S. al Coda 𝄋

I'm

(to Coda)

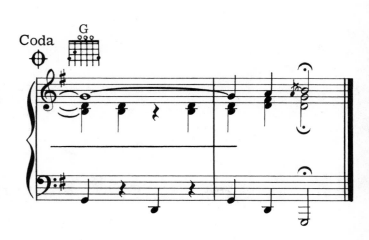

Coda ⊕

Please Daddy
(Don't Get Drunk This Christmas)

Words and Music by Bill Danoff and Taffy Nivert

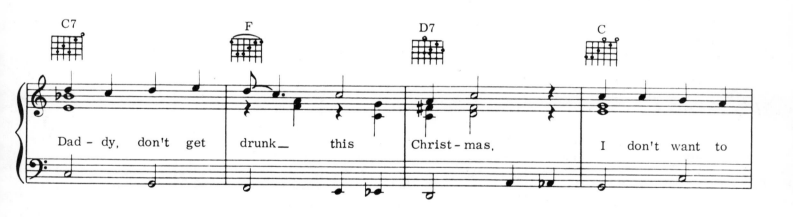

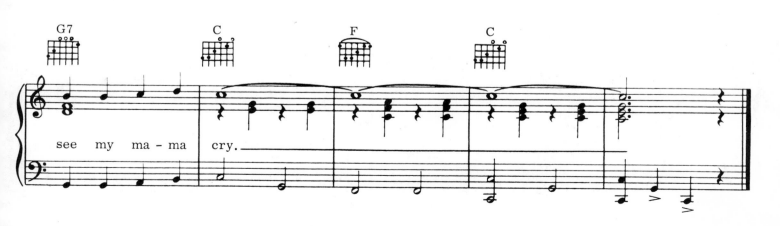

River Of Love

Words and Music by John Martin Sommers

be - come__ some-one__ else - 's bride.__
dar - lin' won't you come back__ home__ a - gain.__
nev - er ev - er see your__ smile__ a - gain.__

Oh the

riv - er__ of love__ it has__ gone__ mud - dy

and the

flow-ers they are dy - ing on the shore.__

And the

blue skies have all__ turned to dark - ness

and the

night - in-gale___ will sing no___ more.

more.   To-mor- more   And the

blue skies   have all___ turned to   dark-ness_____   and the

night - in-gale___ will sing no___   more._____

Ruby,
Don't Take Your Love To Town

Words and Music by Mel Tillis

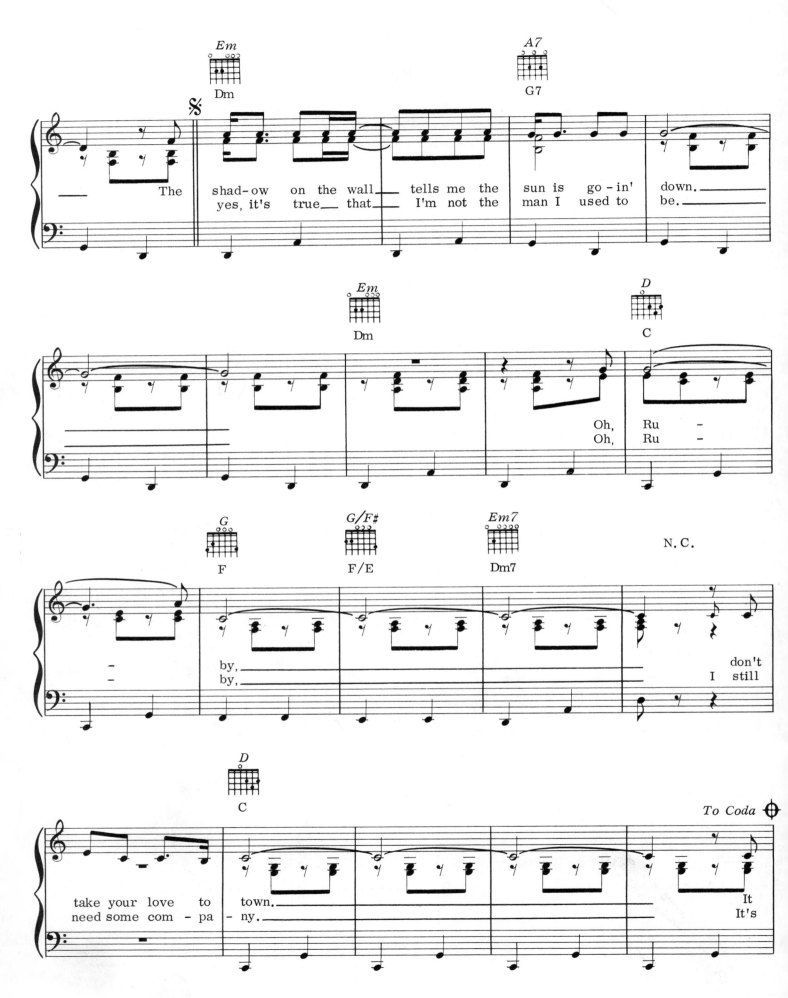

Em
Dm

A7
G7

The shad-ow on the wall___ tells me the sun is go-in' down.___
yes, it's true___ that___ I'm not the man I used to be.___

Em
Dm

D
C

Oh, Ru -
Oh, Ru -

G
F

G/F#
F/E

Em7
Dm7

N.C.

by,___
by,___

don't
I still

D
C

To Coda ⊕

take your love to town.___
need some com - pa - ny.___

It
It's

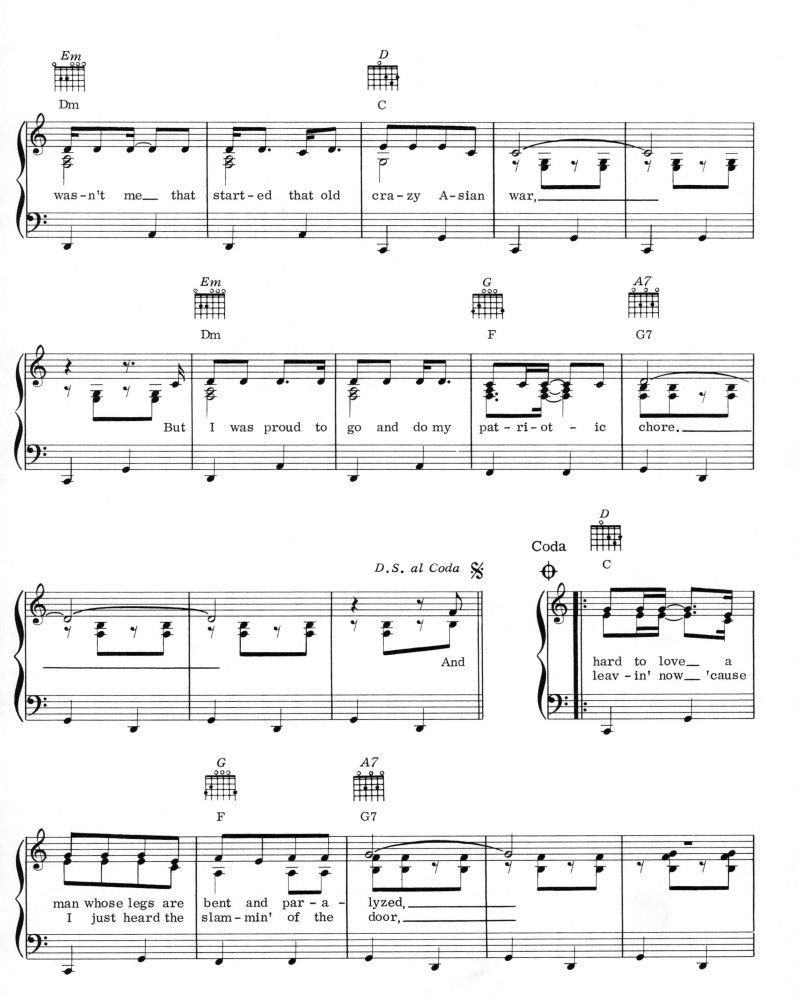

was-n't me___ that start-ed that old cra-zy A-sian war,___

But I was proud to go and do my pat-ri-ot-ic chore.___

D.S. al Coda 𝄋

And

Coda 𝄌

hard to love___ a leav-in' now___ 'cause

man whose legs are bent and par-a-lyzed,___

I just heard the slam-min' of the door,___

She's Got You

Words and Music by Hank Cochran

me!____ I real-ly don't know,_ but I know it won't let me be. I've got your

class ring _____ that_ proved you cared and it still looks the same_ as when you

gave it, dear._ The on-ly thing dif-f'rent,____ the on-ly thing new, I've got these

lit-tle things,_ she's got you.

Susan When She Tried

Words and Music by Don Reid

Sweet Music Man

Words and Music by Kenny Rogers

I won't be there to hold your hand like I used to;___ I'm through___ with you.___

You're a hell of a sing - er and a pow-er-ful man,___ but you sur-

round___ your-self___ with peo - ple who de-mand so lit-tle of you.___

You touched my soul with your beau-ti-ful song,___

You e - ven had___ me sing-in' a - long___ right

no-bod-y else could make___ me feel___ that things are right___ when I know___ they're wrong.___

No-bod-y sings a love___ song___ quite like you.

Verse 2

Sing your song, sweet mu-sic man,___ You

trav-el the world___ with a six piece band___ that does___ for you what you

ask 'em to. And you try to stay young but the songs you've sung to

so man-y peo-ple they've all be-gun to come back on you.

So sing your song, sad mu-sic man,

You're mak-in' your liv - in' do-in' one-night stands that

prove to you they don't need you. You're still a

233

hell of a sing-er but a brok-en man,_ but you'll keep on look-in' for one last fan to

sing 'em to.__ But no-bod-y sings a love_song quite like

Chorus

you do,_____ And no-bod-y else could make_ me sing a- long,____ And

no-bod-y else could make_ me feel_ that things are right_when I know_ they're wrong._

235

Take Me Home, Country Road

Words and Music by Bill Danoff, Taffy Nivert and John Denver

236

young - er than the moun - tains___ grow - in' like a breeze.___
mist - y taste of moon - shine,___ tear - drop in my eye.___

Coun - try Roads,_____ take me home_____ to the

place_____ I be - long:_____ West Vir - gin - ia,_____

moun - tain mom - ma,_____ Take me home,_____ Coun - try

Roads._____ All my I hear her voice, in the

morn - in' hours she calls___ me, the ra - di - o re - minds me of my

home far a - way, and driv - in' down the road I get a feel - in' that I

should have been home yes - ter - day,___ yes - ter - day.___

D.S. %al Coda ⊕

Coda ⊕

Roads,_____ take me home,_____ Coun - try Roads,_____

_____ take me home,_____ Coun - try Roads._____

Ten More Nights
In This Old Barroom

Words and Music by Pat and Victoria Garvey

Waltz tempo

Ten more___ nights_____ in this old___ bar-room,

Lake Chi-ca-go's got me down.

Ten more__ nights_____ in this old__ bar - room,
run - ning____ me rag - ged and run - ning me____
down. Eve - ning sounds are
lone - ly sounds, but the lone - li - est of

241

Teddy Bear

Words and Music by Dale Royal, Billy Joe Burnette, Red Sovine and Tommy Hill

Moderately bright

(RECITATION:) I was on the outskirts of a little southern town; trying to reach my destination before the sun went down... The CB was blaring away on channel 19... when there came a little boy's voice on the radio line... He said: "Breaker 19!... Is anyone there? Come on back, truckers... and talk to Teddy Bear!"... I keyed the mike and said: "You got it, Teddy Bear!" And a little boy's voice came back on the air... "'Preciate the break,... Who we got on that end?"... I told him my handle and he began: ...

"I'm not supposed to bother you fellows out there... Mom says you're busy and for me to stay off the air... But you see, I get lonely and it helps to talk... 'cause that's all I can do... I'm crippled,... I can't walk!!!"

I came back and told him to fire up that mike... and I'd talk to him as long as he liked... "This was my dad's radio" the little boy said... "But I guess it's mine and mom's now, 'cause my dad's dead!"

"He had a wreck about a month ago... He was trying to get home in a blinding snow... Mom has to work now, to make ends meet... and I'm not much help with my two crippled feet!"

"She says not to worry... that we'll make it alright... But I hear her crying sometimes late at night... There's just one thing I want more than anything to see... Aw, I know you guys are too busy to bother with me!"

"But my dad used to take me for rides when he was home... but that's all over now, since my daddy's gone..."... Not one breaker came on the old CB as the little crippled boy talked with me... I tried to swallow a lump that wouldn't stay down... as I thought about my boy back in Greenville Town.

"Dad was going to take mom and me with him later on this year... I remember him saying: 'Someday this old truck will be yours, Teddy Bear!'... But I know now I will never get to ride an 18 wheeler again... but this old bas will keep me in touch with all my trucker friends!"

"Teddy Bear's gonna back on out now and leave you alone 'cause it's about time for Mom to come home... Give me a shout when you're passing through... and I'll surely be happy to come back to you!"

I came back and said: "Before you go, 10-10... what's your home 20, little CB friend?"... He gave me his address and I didn't once hesitate... this hot load of freight would just have to wait!

I turned that truck around on a dime and headed for Jackson Street, 229... I round the corner and got one heck of a shock... 18 wheelers were lined up for three city blocks!

Every driver for miles around had caught Teddy Bear's call... and that little crippled boy was having a ball... For as fast as one driver would carry him in, another would carry him to his truck and take off again.

Well, you better believe I took my turn riding Teddy Bear... and then carried him back in and put him down on his chair... And if I never live to see happiness again... I saw it that day in the face of that little man.

We took up a collection for him before his mama got home... Each driver said goodbye and then they were gone... He shook my hand with his mile-long grin and said: "So long, trucker... I'll catch you again!"

I hit the Interstate with tears in my eyes... I turned on the radio and got another surprise... "Breaker 19!" Came the voice on the air... "Just one word of thanks from Mama Teddy Bear!"

"We wish each and every one a special prayer for you... you made a little crippled boy's dream come true... I'll sign off now, before I start to cry... May God ride with you... 10-4... and goodbye!"

Thank God I'm A Country Boy

Moderately

Words and Music by John Martin Sommers

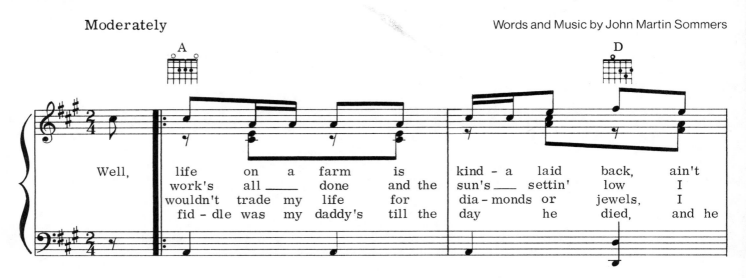

Well, life on a farm is kind-a laid back, ain't
work's all ____ done and the sun's ____ settin' low I
wouldn't trade my life for dia-monds or jewels, I
fid-dle was my daddy's till the day he died, and he

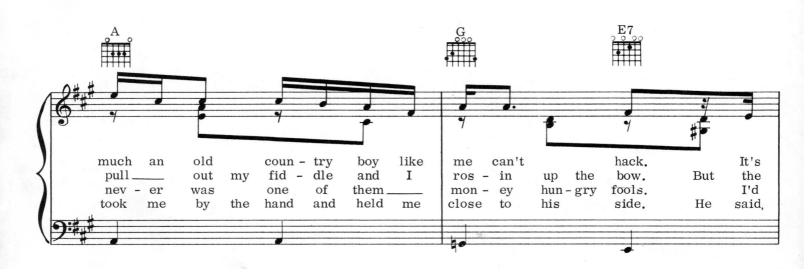

much an old coun-try boy like me can't hack. It's
pull ____ out my fid-dle and I ros-in up the bow. But the
nev-er was one of them ____ mon-ey hun-gry fools. I'd
took me by the hand and held me close to his side. He said,

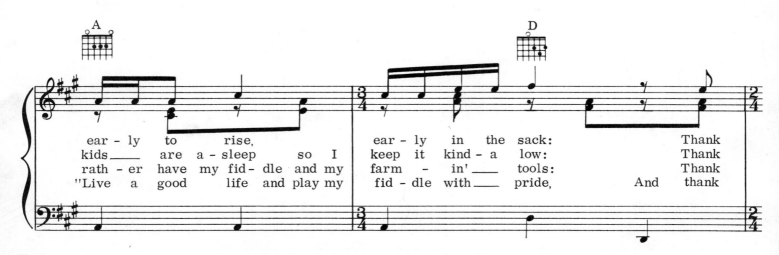

ear-ly to rise, ear-ly in the sack: Thank
kids ____ are a-sleep so I keep it kind-a low: Thank
rath-er have my fid-dle and my farm-in' ____ tools: Thank
"Live a good life and play my fid-dle with ____ pride, And thank

245

got me a fine wife, I got me old fid-dle. When the

sun's com-in' up I got cakes___ on the grid-dle; And

life ain't noth-in' but a fun-ny, fun-ny rid-dle:___ Thank

(4th time only)

(4th time)

God I'm a coun-try boy.___

1. 2. 3.

4.

2. When the
3. I
4. Well, my

246

Torn Between Two Lovers

Words and Music by Peter Yarrow and Phillip Jarrell

247

248

Today I Started Loving You Again

Words and Music by Merle Haggard and Bonnie Owens

With on - ly these few mil-lion tears I've cried.

I should have known_____ the worst_____ was yet_____ to

come_____ And that cry - in' time_____ for

me_____ had just be - gun._____ Well, to-

D.S. al Coda

Waterloo

Words and Music by John D. Loudermilk and Marijohn Wilkin

where old Ad - am met his Wa - ter - loo.
where Na - po - leon met his Wa - ter - loo.
where Tom Doo - ley met his Wa - ter - loo.

Wa - ter -

Chorus

loo, Wa - ter - loo, Where will you meet your Wa - ter -

loo? Ev - 'ry pup - py has its day, ev - 'ry - bod - y has to pay, Ev - 'ry -

bod - y has to meet his Wa - ter - loo.

last time, slower

2. Lit - tle loo.

3. Now a

Whatever Happened To Randolph Scott

Words and Music by Don Reid and Harold Reid

Chorus

257

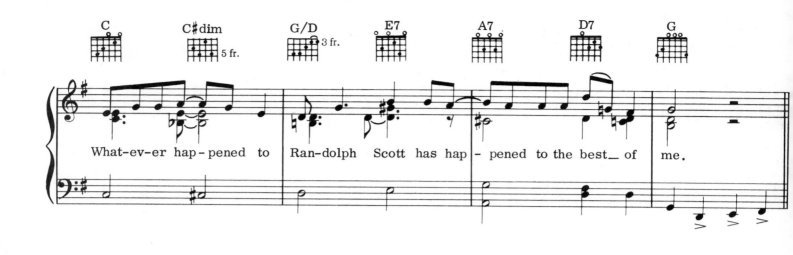

What-ev-er hap-pened to Ran-dolph Scott has hap-pened to the best__ of me.

N.C.

Verse 2

Ev-'ry-bod-y's try-ing to make a com-ment a-bout our doubts and fears. "True

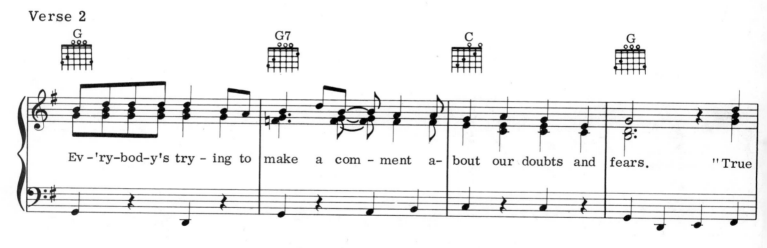

Grit's" the on-ly mov-ie I've real-ly un-der-stood in years.__ You

got-ta take_ your | an-a-lyst a-long to | see if it's fit to | see.

What-ev-er hap-pened to | Ran-dolph Scott has | hap-pened to the in-dus- | try.

Chorus

What-ev-er hap-pened to | John-ny Mack Brown and_ | Al-lan Rock-y | Lane?

What-ev-er hap-pened to | Lash La-rue,_ I'd_ | love to see them a - | gain.

Wildwood Flower

Adapted and Arranged by Dan Fox

With the myr - tle as bright as the
How my heart is now won - d'ring no
I have woke from my dream and my

F   C
em - er - ald dew,
mis - 'ry can tell,   The
i - dol is clay   He
                                       All

                        G7
ghost - ly pale rid - er   with eyes of bright
left with no warn - ing,   no word of fare -
por - tions of love   have flown far a -

1. 2. C   3. C
blue._____   2. Oh, he   way.
well._____   3. I will

8 - - - - - -

When I Was Young

Words and Music by Jim Friedman and Sue Cahn

round each mist-y rain-bow bend___ and won-dered where and when__ your game would

a tempo

end. At last you came to rest,__ my wan-d'ring one,___ A hope with-

in my breast,__ a song half sung. And now I won-der, when__ the song is

more broadly

sung,___ If you'll be what you were__ when I was young.

slower

Wolverton Mountain

Words and Music by Merle Kilgore and Claude King

Chorus

Clow - ers_____ has a pret-ty young daugh - ter;_____ He's might - y
chanc - es_____ and_ climb_ that moun - tain,_____ Though Clif - ton
right_____ to_ hide_ his daugh - ter _____ From___ the

han - dy_____ with a gun_ and a knife._____
Clow - ers,_____ he may take_ my_ life._____
one_____ who_ loves_ her_ so._____

Her ten - der lips _____ are sweet - er than
mp - mf

hon - ey_____ And Wol - ver - ton Moun - tain _____

protects her there. The bears and birds tell Clif - ton Clow - ers If a stran - ger should wan - der there. 2. All of my 3. I'm go - ing there. But I don't

269

You've Never Been This Far Before

Words and Music by Conway Twitty

feel your bod - y | trem - ble | as you | won - der what this | mo - ment holds_ in_
know and I don't | care what | made you | tell him you don't | love him an - y -

store, | bum, bum, bum._ | | And as I
more. | | | And as I

put my arms a - | round_you | I can tell | you've nev - er | been this far_ be -
taste your ten - der | kiss - es, | I can tell | |
hope that you'll be - | lieve_me | 'cause I | know |

To Coda ✛

fore, | bum, bum, bum._ | | **1.** I don't | **2.** And as I

take the love you're giv-ing I can feel the ten-sion build-ing in your
won-d'ring if to-mor-row I'll still love you like I'm lov-ing you to-

mind,
night.

hum, hum, hum.

1. And you're

2. You

have no way of know-ing but to-night will on-ly make me love you more.

D. S. al Coda

And I

Coda

bum, bum, bum.

Yesterday When I Was Young
(Hier Encore)

English lyric by Herbert Kretzmer
Original French text and music by Charles Aznavour

Moderately

Gm7   C7   Fmaj7

Yes-ter- day_____ when I was young, The taste of life was sweet as rain up-on my
day_____ the moon was blue, And ev-'ry cra-zy day brought some-thing new to

Bbmaj7   Em7-5   A7

tongue,   I teased at life as if   it were a fool-ish game,   The way the eve-ning
do,   I used my mag-ic age   as if it were a wand,   And nev-er saw the

Dm   Gm7

breeze   may tease a can-dle flame;   The thou-sand dreams I dreamed, The splen-did things I
waste   and emp-ti-ness be- yond;   The game of love I played with ar-ro-gance and

273

Index of Composers and Lyricists